The Rule of Saint Benedict

Abbot Parry OSB
&
Esther de Waal

Gracewing.

First published in 1990
Reprinted 1990, 1993, 1995, 1997, 2000 & 2003

Gracewing
2 Southern Avenue, Leominster
Herefordshire HR6 0QF

ISBN 978-1-78182-018-6

Additional typesetting by Action Publishing Technology Ltd,
Gloucester GL1 5SR

I am writing these instructions to you, so that . . . you may know how to behave in the household of God.

I Tim 3:14–15 (RSV)

. . . so that no one may be upset or saddened in the household of God.

The Rule of St Benedict (Ch.31)

Preface

'Who is the man who desires to see Good Days?' Normally when a young man or a young woman decides to enter a monastery, friends and relatives do not immediately conclude that he or she is seeking a good time. They are more likely to think that their friend takes a poor view of life's possibilities. Yet in the Prologue to the Rule we find St Benedict quoting the Scripture: 'Who is the man who desires life and is eager to see Good Days?' (Ps 33:12). Evidently he believes that he has something of real value to offer, and he continues: 'What can be sweeter to us than the voice of the Lord as he invites us, dearest brothers? See how in his loving mercy the Lord points out to us the Way of Life.' The expression recalls how Christ called himself the Way (Jn 14:6) and the earliest Christians referred to themselves simply as followers of the Way (Acts 9:2). Before we examine St Benedict's exposition of how to follow the Way, a few words on the man himself may be useful.

The traditional dates for the life of St Benedict are 480–547. The only early account of his life that we have is that given by St Gregory, Pope, 590–604. St Gregory drew information from persons who had known St Benedict personally. But the concept of how to write a biography differed so much in the sixth century from what we expect in the twentieth that St Gregory's account is today accepted only with considerable reserve. Moreover a careful examination of what he does tell us is leading some modern scholars[1] to place St Benedict's life rather

[1] *La Règle de Saint Benoît* (1980) tr. and ed. H. Rochais and E. Manning. Paris, Edition du Centenaire, Desclée de Brouwer, 1980.

later, say about 520–575. The salient outline is not in dispute.

Born of an honourable family of Nursia in Tuscany, he studied in his youth at Rome. Disgusted by the decadent culture that he found there, he departed, still very young, seeking God in solitude in the mountains round Subiaco, fifty miles to the west of Rome. While he was still quite young, a local monastery invited him to be its abbot. He accepted, but the experiment did not last long, and he willingly returned to his solitude. There disciples came to him and he became the founder of a monastery, and lived, it seems, in the ruins of Nero's villa, bordering on a lake (Sub-lacu). A second time he encountered opposition, this time apparently from outside the monastery. So he migrated southward and established himself on Monte Cassion, overlooking the road between Rome and Naples. Here, making extensive use of materials already in existence, he composed the Rule on which his fame rests.

If we want to know his personality it is really to this document we must turn. Its Prologue shows that the youthful urge to brook no delay, which had led him to abandon his Roman studies, still lived on in the mature man. For him, 'the way of God's Commandments' is 'run in a sweetness of love that is beyond words', and the Gospel command 'Walk while you have the light' (Jn 12:35) appears in the Prologue changed, no doubt unconsciously, into 'Run while you have the light.'

We may note here that a modern reader perusing the Rule for the first time might conclude from the mass of Scripture texts fired at him, that St Benedict lacked originality. It is well then to underline that if this man is always quoting Scripture it is because its teachings and its very words have become the texture of his mind. His invariable approach to every problem is to ask: 'What does the Lord say about this?' And for him that is the key to the answer. Hence he expresses his doctrine quite naturally by weaving together those scriptural texts which have formed his mind.

Although we think of St Benedict as a founder, if only because the majority of those who follow his Rule are called Benedictines, in reality his position in history is not as simple as that. The monastic life had already had a history of two hundred years, and in his day it was already widespread in both the Eastern and Western parts of the Church. Benedict then entered the ranks of an existing institution and produced a rule based on his knowledge of what was happening around him as well as on his own experience at Subiaco and Monte Cassino. The text which he left behind him was seen as a *Summa* of the best monastic wisdom of his day, and it would remain a central document by which future generations of monks would guide themselves.

The reader who does not belong to the monastic order, but reads the Rule as one among other spiritual classics, may find it by comparison with other inspired spiritual writings rather a matter-of-fact document. It is indeed a restrained and balanced one, but to understand it the reader must accept its point of view. It is not just spiritual teaching, nor just a personal code, but it aims to set up a whole society (if a small one) that is truly Christ-centred, and provided with the legislation that will, as far as any legislation can, keep it on course. This requires both depth of spiritual teaching and a balanced recognition of the needs of human nature. If it has survived for so many centuries, its survival is due to the combination of the two elements: experience of the actualities of human life in community and the insights of one to whom 'nothing is to be preferred to Christ'. St Benedict brought both characteristics to bear in constructing his 'household of God'.

The Rule is not intended to displace in any way the Gospel from the centre of the way of life of this monastic society. On the contrary the Gospel is the supreme rule. 'It is under its guidance that we pursue our way' (Prol.), and the function of the Rule is to enable us to apply the fullness of the Gospel teaching to the actual circumstances of daily life, not only on the level of the response of the individual, but also through the attitude of society. For this purpose it draws heavily on previous experience and on the writings of the Fathers of the Church.

Experience teaches negative as well as positive lessons. And the first Chapter of the Rule takes a look round the monastic world as St Benedict saw it in his day. He found a good deal in which the results did not correspond to the ideal. So the Rule discarded much that was seen to have no permanent value, and set out to build a monastery that would be both solid and fruitful in its spiritual formation. The quest for stability is basic to its thinking: yet it presented a balance of flexibility largely because it left a wide sphere open to the judgement of the Abbot, and so could remain a usable guide through all succeeding centuries until this one. Indeed, in different ages and places one may observe major departures from what the Rule laid down; yet sooner or later there is a return to a closer interpretation. It is perhaps through this rhythm in which adaptation and a return to the closer observance follow each other, that each succeeding generation of monks keeps the Rule alive in history. It is not a matter of alternations of strictness and laxity in observance, but of adaptation, greater or less, to the climate of the spiritual world of each age or to the local needs of the Church.

In constructing the society, Benedict follows a three-fold line of thought.

Firstly, he is a teacher of monastic doctrine. As we have already said, this doctrine did not supplant the Gospel. At this level the Rule embodies certain maxims laid down as a fruit of experience, and certain virtues without which the pursuit of the Gospel would be an illusion and the desire for union with God a path of self-deception. There was nothing new in the teachings; it was the fruit of experience: thus the longest Chapter of the Rule (VII) is about Humility and the theme runs through all the others. Another equally radical chapter is on Obedience (V), for the practice of obedience was seen as inseparable from that of humility. A third chapter dealt with the practice of Silence (VI). This may seem a more technical matter, but it was seen as a safeguard to the practice of other necessary things (recollection in prayer) both for the individual and the society as a whole. A lengthy chapter on 'The Tools of Good Works' (IV) may seem to contain much that is obvious from both the Old and New Testaments, but there are many moments in a man's life when such reminders are more useful than more elevated sentiments.

The reader should note, however, that while spiritual teaching predominates in the earlier chapters, it is not confined to them. Spiritual teaching occurs throughout the Rule even in the most prosaic matters (e.g. Ch. LVII 'The Craftsmen of the Monastery' and Ch. XL 'The Measure of Drink'). The concluding chapters of the Rule are particularly significant in this respect. While the spiritual teaching of the Rule is both rich and balanced, teaching alone does not set up a society.

The second element the Rule provides for is the structure of the House of God: the Abbot as the father; the monks with their equality as brethen (Ch. II); the community to be consulted in grave matters (Ch. III); the senior monks to be consulted in lesser ones. A wide sphere of temporal cares is assigned to the cellarer, with significant instructions (Ch. XXXI); other officials are established, also with appropriate instructions (e.g. Ch. LXVI, 'The Doorkeepers'). There is discussion on the desirability of appointing a Prior (Ch. LXV, the Rule betrays uncertainty here) and the order of the Brethren in community. These and other matters are legislated for, and are clearly of great significance in the construction of the way of life of the monastery. They are still formative in monastic society.

The third strand in the organisation established by the Rule is that of observances. These begin with Ch. VIII, in which chapter and the following ones Benedict lays down in great detail how and when the Divine Office is to be said. This is followed by several chapters of the Penal Code and then more detailed regulations for the monastic day and for various places of the monastery, for the treatment of newcomers, guests etc. Indeed, the central stretch of the Rule ranged through all the practical aspects of how the life is to be carried out. Regulations, however, are often explained by doctrinal teachings, and even when this is not done, such doctrinal reasons are not far to seek. Thus there is to be strict silence after Compline (Ch. XLII); this was undoubtedly thought of, not merely as a rule, but a co-operation with the divine plan, which assigned activity to the day, and intended the night for repose, and therefore for complete silence. The fact that the Rule is read aloud in monasteries (Ch. LXVI) means that even when variations are made, the mind of the legislator can never be forgotten.

The amount of space St Benedict devotes to organising the Divine Office is significant of the importance he attached to it. Nor was it merely a matter of long vocal prayer. For the early monks understood prayer to be the principal means for attaining union with God, and union with God was the end of human living and therefore of the monastic organisation. It should be noted that while Chs. VIII–XX are all about prayer, the subject recurs again and again in the Rule. It is hardly too much to say that it gives meaning to the whole.

The little chapter on when Alleluia is to be said (XV), should not be passed over as insignificant; on the contrary, it reminds us how important the theme of the Resurrection was in the lives of the monks, and how they illustrated this.

For the life of the monk was not just a programme of aspirations for moral improvement. Spiritual progress meant a closer 'incorporation in Christ', and this in turn implied living with the thought of the Paschal Mystery in mind. That Mystery reached its consummation in the Resurrection. So this chapter enacted that the Resurrection should be recalled, as day succeeded day.

The section that is likely to cause most raising of eyebrows to the modern reader is that of the Penal Code (Chs. XXII–XXX). And there is more of it later (Chs. XLIII–XLVI). To understand this at all we have to grasp the point of view of the sixth-century legislator who is organising a young, vigorous society and conscious of the need to protect it against falling away and corruption. To do this he makes use of such means as were current in his day. Nobody would have questioned it then; equally, nobody would want it unadapted now. Yet it should be noted that a society with definite standards of life which it cherishes, does in all ages have to take appropriate action to defend them. We as a society seem to be reaching a period of real weakness today, as we become more uncertain about the structure and standards of our society. The point of view of the Rule is that the standards of community life have to be guarded with great care.

The Rule then combines these three lines of thought. Some chapters are clearly devoted to one rather than to another, but often they are mingled. Always the intention is to provide a framework for the perfect fulfilment of the Gospel.

Here and there the reader will come across brief phrases which are epitomes of doctrine, usually more lapidary in the Latin than it is possible for them to be in English. Thus we read of the arriving guest: 'Every kindness should be shown him' (Ch. LIII, 'Exhibeatur ei omnis humanitas'); of daily work: 'Idleness is the enemy of the soul' (Ch. XLVIII); of prayer: 'Let it be short and pure unless drawn out by divine inspiration' (Ch. XX), or again on prayer: 'If someone wishes to pray, let him go in without hesitation and pray . . . with tears, and the attention of the heart' (Ch. LII); of the brotherhood: 'They should labour with chaste love at the charity of the brotherhood' (Ch. LXXII). One theme in particular should not go unmentioned: the Rule teaches us to recognise Christ in all persons and in all the circumstances of life: in the persons of the Abbot

(Ch. II), of the sick (Ch. XXXVI), of the poor (Ch. LIII), of the guest (Ch. LIII), and so on. And throughout there is an insistence that it is the disposition of the heart that counts rather than the external performance of the deed: this quality turns the Rule into a spiritual guide, as distinct from a set of laws.

The monks for whom the Rule legislated are not to be thought of as simply a gathering of local peasants. Monastic society was classless, but not therefore ignorant. Provision was made for manual work (Ch. XLVIII), but also arts and crafts (Ch. LVII) and a considerable period was allotted daily for spiritual reading ('lectio divina', Ch. XLVIII). A general distribution of books from the library is mentioned as taking place at the beginning of Lent, where thought is also given to those who are unable or unwilling to read, but they are thought of as exceptions (Ch. XLVIII). The normal equipment of the monk included a pen and writing materials. This basic provision for intellectual culture was to have a great development in later ages, and has even led to the impression that learning was a normal attribute of the Benedictine monk.

Thus the three main occupations of the monk's day were: the work of God (a time of mental as well as verbal prayer), the work of the hands (which in fact included all kinds of work) and spiritual reading (in which the mind was applied to study). These three occupations were seen as complementary; they exercised the monk at diverse levels—spiritual, intellectual and bodily, and so gave a balanced unity to each day.

One does not need to be a monk or a nun to find significance in the values of the Rule. There is a value of a society, set up as a stable and permanent unit, with a total indifference to gaining wealth or ease of living. There is the principle by which the individual fulfils himself through union with God, and on the social level, through love and service of his brethren. Ambition, greed, pride, domination, acquisitiveness are all proscribed and barriers laid down against them. It may seem a fearsome programme, but one which is worthy of consideration by a society which trains every individual to get to the top if he can, encourages all the 'haves' of society to acquire yet more, and leaves the co-ordination of its members to be settled by internal warfare. It is a society based on a totally opposite principle: 'By their fruits you shall know them' (Mt 7:20). Monasticism, as every other system run by men, has its failures, but at least it sheds light on the possibilities of a less egoistic society, suggests qualities necessary for social unity and success, and indicates what makes a path to social breakdown inevitable. Benedict himself lived in a time of social confusion and breakdown. No doubt this led him to a constant insistence on stability for his household. But it is not the sociological content that is his main message. That lies in the construction of a household based in its relationships on the divine teaching: 'Seek first his kingdom and its righteousness' (Mt 6:33). Whatever other merits the Rule may have flow from its concentration on that thought. This concentration is summed up at the conclusion of Ch. LXXII: 'They should prefer nothing to Christ. May he bring us all alike to life everlasting.'

Note

The traditional days of the year have been added in the margin for the benefit of any communities which may wish to use the text for reading aloud.

INTRODUCTION

'Listen my son to the instructions of your Master, turn the ear of your heart to the advice of a loving father.'

These, the opening words of the Rule of St. Benedict, instantly capture our attention. These are the words of a loving father. Already Benedict has revealed his purpose: his Rule is all about love.

It is a practical guide to help men and women establish and maintain loving relationships with God, with others, with the material world, and also (perhaps surprisingly to those who associate Christianity, and in particular monasticism, with denial and asceticism) with one's own self. It is the whole person that is addressed in the Rule of St. Benedict. The whole God-given human being made up of body, mind and spirit. The Rule is written for a life which recognises that these three elements should be accepted and affirmed in a daily rhythm of prayer, study and work, alternating activities that make up that balanced life for which Benedictines are rightly renowned.

This balance, this *via media*, can be to some extent explained by Benedict's own life and character. Born around 480 in Nursia in Italy, in the years in which the Roman Empire and all its certainties were crumbling, he went to university in Rome but then fled in order to pursue the life of a hermit in a cave at Subiaco. Later he came to Monte Cassino where he founded a community of monks where he lived until his death in 547. Thus he knew from his own experiences both the life of a hermit and the life in community. He himself was both moderate and passionate. He wrote with *gravitas* and balance, as the last of the Romans, but he also brought the urgency of the charismatic preacher on fire with a message of fervent love.

The word Rule itself can sometimes be misleading to those unfamiliar with the spiritual realities of the Benedictine life. Benedict tells us to listen with 'the ear of your heart'. His concern in the Rule is always with the disposition of the heart itself. It is, as a contemporary Benedictine puts it, not a series of prescribed actions but a series of opening doors, an invitation to remain alert to the challenge of the Word itself.

'Who is the man who desires life and is eager to see Good Days?'

Right at the start of the Rule we are given a vivid picture of the Lord in the market place calling out to passers by with this offer of fullness of life (Prologue). Here is the possibility of a return, a change, a *metanoia*, for all those who have strayed 'through the slough of disobedience'. That way is bound to be narrow at the start but if we hold on with patience and perseverence, and above all with obedience, then the promise is that:

'through the continual practice of monastic observance and the life of faith, our hearts are opened wide, and the way of God's commandments is run in a sweetness of love that is beyond words' (Prologue).

When Benedict came to write his Rule there were already other monastic texts available, and many people were already living the monastic life. Basically people belonged to one of two groups. Either they were eremetical (seeking God in silence and solitude), or they were coenobetic (seeking God in the common life under the authority of an *abba*, a father). Modestly Benedict described his own effort as a little rule for beginners and told his followers to read further in both these existing (and largely contradictory) traditions (Chapter 73).

But he was of course far too modest. For his compilation brings together the insights of both directions brilliantly and with such flexibility that for 1,500 years his Rule has continued to nurture and inspire men and women. It remains a spring or source to which both individuals and institutions can return time and again to find practical help and guidance, to be both reassured and challenged, to renew their vision.

Perhaps it is useful to see it as containing different levels of writing, a hierarchy of truths. There is the great ringing declaration of the Prologue, Chapter 72 with its panegyric on love, Chapter 7 with its profound exploration of humility, being earthed in the reality of self knowledge. But because it is also essentially a working document, legislation for the common shared life of a group of men (and we know from the Dialogues of St Gregory the Great AD 590-604, how disparate a group Benedict gathered around him at Monte Cassino) many of the chapters are concerned with minutiae which today make tedious, sometimes apparently irrelevant, reading. It is important to recognise this and see beyond it. It is in fact ironically just because it is so mundane and so concrete that the Rule continues to speak so forcibly.

Benedict does not deal in moral abstractions. Instead we are shown real life situations, the rota of kitchen servers (Chapter 35), the porter at the gate (Chapter 66) or the cellarer (bursar) handing out goods (Chapter 31). These confront us with the necessity of finding God, and practising love, in the ordinary, the commonplace, the unspectacular. It is precisely its specifity that makes the Rule so immediate and so inescapable. In its pages we see the radical demands of the Gospel in daily living.

Much of the Rule is taken up with practical discussions of the ordering of life. That is not because Benedict believed that good order is important for its own sake but because he knew that in a well ordered community it is easier to make space and time for God. When he declares that the oratory is the place set aside for prayer and should be used for nothing else (Chapter 52) he is establishing an important principle. He knows that certainty and a firm structure in externals provides a framework and a freedom, in which it becomes more possible to find a place for God. At the end of those chapters (8-18) which have dealt in considerable detail with the ordering of the Psalms he then says that if we can do better we are at liberty to try it (Chapter 18 V. 22). It is not the detail but the principle: muddle and confusion are to be avoided at all costs.

That offer of life in the Prologue comes from the Psalms (Psalm 33.12). It is, as is so much of the Rule, citation from Scripture. A quick glance at the text shows that there are in fact no less than 130 actual Biblical quotations within it. For Benedict is a man seized by the Word, shaped by it, his whole thought so totally formed by it that all he writes comes out of this deep knowledge and love of the Bible. Often the allusions are subtle, as when the cellarer is described as *non turbulentus* (not excitable) a reference to the suffering servant. Above all Benedict loves the Psalms and that is what he would wish for all who follow him. The saying of the daily offices centre on listening to the Word. This is the *opus dei*, the work of God, the life of prayer which is where the Rule is leading us. The corporate prayer is there to uphold a continuing awareness of the presence of God which makes praying inseparable from living, and living from praying.

Written as a guide for life in community, living at close quarters with other people, that most demanding of the human situations, Benedict takes as his starting point the worth of each and every person (Chapter 40). The Abbot handles everyone with a sensitivity that recognises the level at which they will develop to their full potential (Chapter 2). He is of course not only the exemplar of Christ to the brothers but also the example for each of us in our relations with others.

We are shown this in practice in all its ordinariness and dailiness, in the kitchen (Chapter 35) in the infirmary (Chapter 36), how the brothers quietly encourage one another as they get up (Chapter 22) and how lovingly they greet each other when they meet (Chapter 63). So finally when in Chapter 72 we are given that great exposition on love it only draws together all that has been explored earlier about the living out of love in day to day encounters.

The reverence and respect for persons is also found in the reverence and respect for material things. In fact the two are parallel: the job description for the cellarer, the man who handles the goods and property of the monastery is taken from the job description for a bishop (Chapter 31). Chapter 32 has much to say about the careful and responsible handling of tools entrusted to us, just as Chapter 4 lists the tools of the spiritual craft, and we must like faithful stewards return both in due time. For everything is on loan. When monks are told in Chapter 33 that they have nothing of their own that does not mean simply non-possession, it is more fundamental. It is their attitude that they consider nothing as private property. Here is a delicately crafted theology, in which the attitude towards our talents and possessions and towards people all inter- relate. This is one of Benedict's greatest gifts, for he is showing us the possibility of the totality and wholeness inherent in all of life.

Benedict's grasp of the human psyche, and his knowledge of the human predicament, is such that he speaks to all of us, his message is universal. When the novice on entering the community lays the three vows on the altar and says *Suscipe me (Accept me* Lord according to your word) that prayer and these vows reflect basic human needs. Stability is in essence a commitment to not trying to run away, to escape from the place in which one finds oneself; *conversatio morum* a commitment to continual conversion, to follow the call of Christ wherever it may lead; obedience, a commitment to hearing the voice of God and responding with a willing Yes.

These vows tell us much about ourselves on our journey to God, and about our relations with others; the need to stand firm but also to live open to change, and all the time to listen to God reaching out to us. But they also, like the whole Rule of St. Benedict itself, point us forwards towards the figure of Christ. Christ is the rock on whom we build. Christ is the way we follow. Christ is the word we hear.

'... prefer nothing whatever to Christ. May he bring us all alike to life everlasting' (Chapter 72).

This ultimately is the whole message of the Rule. It was a message that came through clearly to Benedict's own community, and it is a message that still comes through clearly to us today some 15 centuries later.

Esther de Waal

The Rule of Saint Benedict

Contents of The Rule of St Benedict

Appendix

Epilogue

The Prologue

1 • Listen my son to the instructions of your Master, turn Jan. 1
the ear of your heart to the advice of a loving father; May 2 Sept. 1
2 accept it willingly and carry it out vigorously; • so that
through the toil of obedience you may return to him from
whom you have separated by the sloth of disobedience.[1]
3 • To you, then, whoever you may be, are my words
addressed, who, by the renunciation of your own will, are
taking up the strong and glorious weapons of obedience
in order to do battle in the service of the Lord Christ, the
true King.
4 • First of all, whenever you begin any good work, you
must ask of God with the most urgent prayer that it may
5 be brought to completion by him, • so that he, who has
now deigned to reckon us in the number of his sons, may
6 not later on be made sad by our wicked actions. • For we
must at all times use the good gifts he has placed in us, so
that he will not later on disinherit us as an angry father
7 disinherits his sons; • nor like a feared lord, who has been
roused to anger by our sins, hand over to eternal
punishment us wicked slaves for refusing to follow him to
glory.
8 • Let us then at last arouse ourselves, even as Jan. 2
Scripture incites us in the words, 'Now is the hour for us May 3 Sept. 2
9 to rise from sleep.'[2] • Let us, then, open our eyes to the
divine light, and hear with our ears the divine voice as it
10 cries out to us daily. • 'Today if you hear his voice, do not
11 harden your hearts,'[3] • and again, 'He who has ears to
hear, let him hear what the Spirit says to the Churches.'[4]
12 • And what does the Spirit say? 'Come, my sons, listen to

[1] cf. Bar 4:28 [2] Rom 13:11 [3] Ps 94:8 [4] Rev 2:7

me; I shall teach you the fear of the Lord.'[5] • 'Run while 13
you have the light of life lest the darkness of death
overwhelm you.'[6]

Jan. 3
May 4
Sept. 3

• And as the Lord seeks his workman in the mass of 14
people, he again cries out to him in the words, • 'Who is 15
the man who desires life and is eager to see Good Days?'[7]
• If you hear this and reply, 'I do', God says to you, • 'If 16,
you want to have true and everlasting life, keep your
tongue from speaking evil, and your lips from uttering
deceit. Turn aside from evil and do good; seek peace and
follow after it.'[8] • 'When you do this my eyes will be 18
upon you, and my ears will be open to your prayers, and
before you call upon me I shall say to you: "Here I
am".'[9] • What can be sweeter to us than this voice of the 19
Lord as he invites us, dearest brothers? • See how, in his 20
loving mercy, the Lord points out to us the Way of Life.[10]

Jan. 4
May 5
Sept. 4

• Let us therefore make for ourselves a girdle out of 21
faith and perseverance in good works, and under the
guidance of the Gospel let us pursue our way in his
paths, so that we may deserve to see him who has called
us to his Kingdom. • For if we wish to make our home in 22
the dwelling-place of his Kingdom, there will be no
getting there unless we run towards it by good deeds.
• But let us question the Lord with the prophet, saying to 23
him, 'Lord, who shall make his home in your dwelling-
place; who shall rest on your holy mountain?'[11] • And 24
then let us listen to the Lord's answer to our question, as
he shows us the way to this dwelling-place, • saying, 'He 25
who walks without fault and does what is right; • he who 26
tells the truth in his heart; he who works no deceit with
his tongue; • he who does no wrong to his neighbour; he 27

---

[5] Ps 33:13 [6] cf. Jn 12:35 [7] Ps 33:12 [8] ibid 14-15 [9] cf. Is 58:9 [10] Ps 25:10; Ac 9:2; 19:9, 23
[11] Ps 14:1

28 who does not slander his neighbour.'[12] • 'He who casts
the wicked devil, even as he beguiles him, out of the sight
of his heart, along with the temptation itself, and so
reduces him to impotence, and takes the incipient
thoughts that he suggests and dashes them against (the
29 rock of) Christ';[13] • those who fear the Lord and do not
become conceited about keeping the law well, but realise
that the good in themselves cannot be their own work but
30 is done by the Lord, • and who praise the Lord
working within them, as they say with the prophet, 'Not
unto us, Lord, not unto us, but unto your name, give the
31 glory.'[14] • For neither did the Apostle Paul give himself
any credit for his preaching, but said, 'By the grace of
32 God I am what I am.'[15] • And the same Apostle also
said, 'He who boasts must boast in the Lord.'[16]

33 • And so the Lord also says in the Gospel, 'Everyone Jan. 5
who listens to these words of mine and acts on them, will May 6 Sept. 5
be like a sensible man who built his house on rock;
34 • floods rose, gales blew and hurled themselves against
that house, and it did not fall; it was founded on rock.'[17]
35 • Thus the Lord concludes his reply, and daily expects us
to respond through our dutiful actions to his holy
precepts.

36 • Therefore in order that amends may be made for
sins, the days of our life are prolonged to give us a time
37 in which to make our piece, • as the Apostle says, 'Do
you realise that the patience of God is meant to lead you
38 to repentance?'[18] • For this loving Lord says, 'I do not
wish the death of the sinner, but that he should change
his ways and live.'[19]

39 • We have asked the Lord, my brothers, about the Jan. 6
May 7 Sept. 6

---

[12] Ps 2,3 [13] Ps 136:9 [14] Ps 113:1 [15] 1 Co 15:10 [16] II Co 10:17 [17] Mt 7:25 [18] Rm 2:4
[19] Ezk 33:11

kind of man who dwells in his house, and we have heard
what is required in order to do so. So let us fulfil the task
of such a dweller. • That means that we must make 40
ready our hearts and bodies to engage in the warfare of
holy obedience to his commands, • and because our 41
nature has not power to do this, we must ask God to send
forth the help of his grace to our aid. • And, if we wish to 42
escape the punishment of hell and reach eternal life,
• then while there is still time, while we are still living in 43
this body and this life gives us the light to do all these
things, • we must hurry to do now what will profit us for 44
ever.

Jan. 7 • We propose, therefore to establish a school of the 45
May 8
Sept. 7 Lord's service, • and in setting it up we hope we shall lay 46
down nothing that is harsh or hard to bear. • But if for 47
adequate reason, for the correction of faults or the
preservation of charity, some degree of restraint is laid
down, • do not then and there be overcome with terror, 48
and run away from the way of salvation, for its beginning
must needs be difficult.[20] • On the contrary, through the 49
continual practice of monastic observance and the life of
faith, our hearts are opened wide, and the way of God's
commandments is run in a sweetness of love that is
beyond words. • Let us then never withdraw from 50
discipleship to him, but persevering in his teachings in
the monastery till death, let us share the sufferings of
Christ through patience, and so deserve also to share in
his kingdom.

[20] Mt 7:14

Preliminary Survey

Chapter I The Kinds of Monk

1 • It is clear that there are four kinds of monk. Jan. 8
May 9
2 • The first kind are the Cenobites, that is the Sept. 8
'monastery' kind, who do battle under a Rule and an
Abbot.
3 • Then the second kind are the Anchorites or Hermits;
these are they who are no longer in the first fervour of
their religious life but have been tested for a long time in
4 the monastery • and have learnt, with the assistance of
5 many brothers, how to do battle against the devil, • and
now, well equipped to leave the fraternal battle-line for
the solitary combat of the desert, they are strong enough
to do battle against the vices of the body and the mind on
their own, with their own resources, relying on God's
aid, but now without the support of anyone else.
6 • The third kind of monk is the abominable one of Jan. 9
May 10
Sarabaites, who have not been tested by a rule, as gold is Sept. 9
tested in a furnace, nor been taught by experience, but
7 are like soft lead. • They keep faith with this world by
their actions, but manifestly lie to God by their tonsure.
8 • These people live in twos and threes, or even alone;
they have no shepherd, they shut themselves up in their
own sheepfolds, not those of the Lord; and their law
9 consists in yielding to their desires: • what they like or
choose they call holy, and they reckon illicit whatever
displeased them.
10 • The fourth kind of monk are those called Wanderers.
These are never stable throughout their whole lives but
wanderers through diverse regions, receiving hospitality
in the monastic cells of others for three or four days at a
11 time. • Always roving and never settling, they follow

their own wills, enslaved by the attractions of gluttony. They are in all respects worse than the Sarabaites.

• It is better to pass over in silence than to speak 12
further of the unhappy way of life of all these people, • so 13
let us pass them by, and with God's help set about organising the strongest kind of monks—the Cenobites.

1
The Formation and Nature of the Monastery

Chapter II What Kind of Man the Abbot should be

1 • An Abbot who is worthy to be in charge of a monastery Jan. 10 May 11
must always bear in mind what he is called and fulfil in Sept. 10
2 his actions the name of one who is called greater.[1] • For
he is believed to act in the place of Christ in the
3 monastery, since he is called by his title, • as the Apostle
says, 'You have received the Spirit of adoption as sons,
4 through whom we cry, Abba! Father![2] • Therefore the
Abbot should not teach or ordain or command anything
5 that lies outside the Lord's commands, far from it; • but
his commands and his teaching should mingle like
the leaven of divine justice in the mind of his disciples.
6 • The Abbot must always remember that at the fearful
judgement of God two things will be discussed: his own
7 teaching and the obedience of his disciples. • The Abbot
must also realise that whatever lack of fruitfulness the
Father of the family may find in his sheep will be blamed
8 on the shepherd. • And likewise if the shepherd has
laboured with complete diligence over a troublesome and
disobedient flock, and has expended every care over their
9 diseased behaviour, • he will be acquitted in the Lord's
judgement and will say with the prophet, 'I have not
hidden your justice in my heart, but I have spoken of
your truth and saving help';[3] 'but they have contemp-
10 tuously despised me.'[4] • And then finally the penalty of
death will swallow up the sheep who were disobedient to
his care.

11 • When, therefore, anyone takes the name of Abbot, he Jan. 11 May 12
should rule over his disciples with two kinds of teaching; Sept. 11
12 • that is to say, he must show forth all good and holy

[1] Mt 18:4 [2] Rm 8:15 [3] Ps 39:11 [4] Is 1:2

things by his words and even more by his deeds. To apt
disciples he must explain the Lord's teaching by word,
but to those who are hard of heart or simple of mind he
must make clear the divine teaching by his actions. • By 13
his deeds he must make it clear that nothing may be done
which he has taught his disciples to be forbidden, lest
while he preaches to others he should merit rejection
himself, • and God should some day say to him as he 14
sins, 'What business have you reciting my statutes,
standing there mouthing my covenant, since you detest
my discipline, and thrust my words behind you?'[5] • And 15
'you observed the splinter in your brother's eye, and did
not notice the plank in your own?'[6]

Jan. 12 May 13 • The Abbot must not show personal preferences in his 16
Sept. 12 monastery. • He must not be more loving to one than to 17
another, unless he had found him to be more advanced in
good works or in obedience. • A free-born man must not 18
be put before one entering the monastery from slavery,
unless some other reasonable cause exists. • But if it 19
seems to the Abbot that there is good reason for it, let
him do so, and let him do the same about the rank of
anyone. Otherwise let them keep their normal order.
• For whether we are slaves or freemen, we are all one in 20
Christ, and serve on equal terms in the army of one Lord;
'for God has no favourites.'[7] • In regard to rank we find 21
distinction in his eyes only if we are found humble and
better than others in good works. • Therefore the Abbot 22
should show himself equally loving to all, and maintain
discipline impartially according to the merits of each.

Jan. 13 May 14 • In his teaching the Abbot should always observe the 23
Sept. 13 method of the Apostle, 'Employ arguments, appeals and
rebukes.'[8] • He must behave differently at different 24

[5] Ps 49:16, 17 [6] Mt 7:3 [7] Rm 2:11 [8] II Tm 4:2

times, sometimes using threats, sometimes encourage-
ment. He must show the tough attitude of a master, and
25 also the loving affection of a father. • Thus he should
sternly reprimand the undisciplined and unruly, but
entreat the obedient, the meek and the patient to go
forward in virtue; as for the careless and the scornful,
26 we instruct him to rebuke and correct them. • He should
not pretend that he does not see the faults of offenders,
but remember the danger overhanging Eli, priest of
Shiloh and, as best he can, he should cut them out by the
27 roots as soon as they begin to show themselves. • He
should correct upright and intelligent minds with verbal
28 admonitions once or twice, • but the shameless, the thick-
skinned and the proud or disobedient, he should repress
at the very beginning of their sinful ways with the
corporal punishment of blows, bearing in mind what is
29 written, 'The fool is not corrected by words,'[9] • and
again, 'Strike your son with the rod and you will deliver
his soul from death.'[10]

30 • The Abbot should always bear in mind what he is; Jan. 14
31 he should bear in mind what he is called; • and let him May 15 Sept. 14
realise that more is demanded of him to whom more is
entrusted. He must realise also how difficult and arduous
is the task he has undertaken, that of ruling souls and
serving men of many different characters; one, indeed, to
be encouraged, another to be rebuked, another
32 persuaded, • each according to his nature and intelligence. Thus he must adapt and fit himself to all, so that
not only will he not lose any of the flock entrusted to
him, but he will rejoice as his good flock increases.

33 • It is most important that he should not pay greater Jan. 15
attention to transient earthly things that pass away, and May 16 Sept. 15

[9] cf. Pr 19:29 [10] cf. Pr 19:18; 23:14

so fail to recognise or underestimate the salvation of the
souls entrusted to him. • Let him always consider that it 34
is souls that he has undertaken to rule, and for whom he
will give an account. • Moreover, in order that he may 35
not complain of reduced temporal goods, let him
remember the Scripture, 'Seek God's Kingdom first, and his
righteousness, and all these other things will be given
you as well,'[11] • and again, 'Nothing is lacking to those 36
who fear him.'[12] • Let him realise that he who under- 37
takes to rule souls must prepare himself to give an
account. • Whatever the number of brethren under his 38
care, he must understand clearly that he will have to
render an account on the Day of Judgement for all these
souls, in addition, of course, to his own. • Thus as he 39
bears ever in mind the enquiry that will be made on the
shepherd's care of the sheep entrusted to him, the
thought that he takes concerning the accounts to be
rendered for others will make him careful of his own
state. • And so, while he provides by his instructions for 40
the amendment of others, he will be brought also to the
amendment of his own faults.

[11] Mt 7:33 [12] Ps 33:10

Chapter III On summoning the Brethren to Council

1 • Whenever anything important has to be done in the Jan. 16
monastery the Abbot must assemble the whole com- May 17 Sept. 16
2 munity and explain what is under consideration. • When
he had heard the counsel of the brethren, he should give
it consideration and then take what seems to him the best
3 course. • The reason why we say that all should be called
to council is this: It is often to a younger brother that the
4 Lord reveals the best course. • But the brethren must
give their counsel submissively and humbly and not
5 presume stubbornly to defend their opinions. • The
decision should, however, depend mainly on the Abbot's
judgement, and all should be joined in obedience to what
6 he considers the soundest course. • But just as it is fitting
that disciples should obey their master, so it is
incumbent on him to settle everything with foresight and
justice.

7 • In every circumstance, therefore, all should follow Jan. 17
the authority of the Rule, nor is it to be rashly abandoned May 18 Sept. 17
8 by anyone. • No one in the monastery is to follow the
9 prompting of his own heart; • no one is to presume to
argue rudely with the Abbot, or to argue at all outside
10 the monastery. • If anyone does so presume, he must
11 submit to disciplinary measures. • The Abbot himself,
however, in all his actions must fear God and keep the
Rule, bearing in mind that most surely he will have to
render account for all his decisions before God, the most
just judge.

12 • If, however, there are less important matters to be
transacted for the well-being of the monastery, the Abbot
13 should take counsel only with the senior monks, • for it is

written, 'Take counsel about all you do and afterwards you will have no regrets.'[1]

[1] Sir 32:19

Chapter IV The Tools of Good Works

1 • In the first place to love the Lord God with all one's Jan. 18
heart, with all one's soul and with all one's strength.[1] May 19 Sept. 18
2 • Then to love one's neighbour as oneself[2]
3 • Then not to kill
4 • Not to commit adultery
5 • Not to steal
6 • Not to covet
7 • Not to bear false witness
8 • To honour all men[3]
9 • Not to do to another what one would not wish to have done to oneself
10 • To deny oneself in order to follow Christ
11 • To punish one's body
12 • Not to seek pleasures
13 • To love fasting
14 • To relieve the poor
15 • To clothe the naked
16 • To visit the sick
17 • To bury the dead
18 • To give help in trouble
19 • To console the sorrowful
20 • To avoid worldly behaviour
21 • To set nothing before the love of Christ
22 • Not to give way to anger Jan. 19 May 20
23 • Not to cherish an opportunity for displaying one's Sept. 19
anger
24 • Not to preserve deceit in one's heart
25 • Not to give the kiss of peace insincerely
26 • Not to abandon charity

---

[1] Mt 22:37 [2] ibid. 39 [3] 1 P 2:17

• Not to swear, for fear of perjury 27
• To speak with one's mouth the truth that lies in one's 28
heart
• Not to return evil for evil 29
• Not to inflict any injury, but to suffer injuries patiently 30
• To love one's enemies[4] 31
• Not to curse anyone who curses us, but instead to 32
return a blessing
• To suffer persecution for righteousness' sake 33
• Not to be arrogant 34
• Not given to drinking 35
• Not a heavy eater 36
• Not given to much sleeping 37
• Not lazy 38
• Not a grumbler 39
• Not a detractor 40
• To rest one's hope in God 41
• Whenever one perceives any good in oneself to 42
attribute it to God, not to one's self
• But to recognise that whatever is evil is one's own 43
doing, and to blame one's self
Jan. 20 May 21 Sept. 20
• To fear the Day of Judgement[5] 44
• To dread hell 45
• To yearn for eternal life with all possible spiritual 46
desire
• *To keep death daily before one's eyes* 47
• At every moment to keep watch over the actions of 48
one's life
• In every place to know that God most surely beholds 49
one
• To dash the evil thoughts that invade one's heart 50
immediately upon Christ, as upon a rock, and to reveal

---

[4] Mt 5:43 [5] Mt 10:28

them to one's spiritual father
51 • To guard one's mouth against evil and vicious speech
52 • Not to love much talking
53 • Not to utter words that are foolish and provoke laughter
54 • Not to love much or unrestrained laughter
55 • To listen willingly to devout reading
56 • To fall often to prayer
57 • In our daily prayer to God to confess with tears and groans the wrong-doing in our past life
58 • To amend these wrong ways in the future
59 • To reject carnal desires
60 • To hate one's own will
61 • To obey the Abbot's commands in everything, even though he himself (which God forbid) acts otherwise, remembering always that command of the Lord's, 'Do what they tell you, but do not do the things that they do'[6]
62 • To be unwilling to be called holy before one is so, but to be holy first so that it may be truly said of one
63 • To carry out God's commands daily in one's actions Jan. 21 May 22 Sept. 21
64 • To love chastity
65 • To hate no one
66 • Not to cherish bitterness
67 • Not to indulge in envy
68 • Not to love quarelling
69 • To flee vainglory
70 • To revere the elders
71 • To love the young
72 • To pray for one's enemies in the love of Christ
73 • After a quarrel to make peace with the other before sunset
74 • And never to despair of God's mercy

[6] Mt 23:3

• These then are the tools of the spiritual craft. • If we 75, 7
make full use of them unceasingly day and night, then,
when we give them back on the Day of Judgement, we
shall in return receive from the Lord that reward which
he himself has promised, • 'The things that no eye had 77
seen, and no ear has heard, which God has prepared for
those who love him.'[7] • Now the workshop in which we 78
make diligent use of all these tools is the enclosure of the
monastery combined with stability in the community.

[7] I Co 2:9

Chapter V Obedience

1, 2 • The first step in humility is prompt obedience. • This is Jan. 22
fitting for those who hold nothing more dear to them May 23
3 than Christ. • Because they had made profession of holy Sept. 22
service or for fear of hell or to attain the glory of
4 everlasting life, • immediately when something has been
commanded by a superior, it is for them as a divine
command and they cannot allow any delay in its
5 execution. • The Lord says of them, 'As soon as he heard
6 me, he obeyed me.'[1] • And he said also to those who are
to teach, 'Whoever listens to you listens to me.'[2]

7 • Such men, therefore, at once leave whatever they are
8 engaged on, abandon their own will, • and with hands
set free by leaving unfinished what they are doing, with
the quick feet of obedience, follow by action the voice of
9 him who gives the order. • And so it is as if in a single
moment the order of the master is uttered and the work
of the disciple is completed with the speed inspired by
the fear of the Lord. The two things are swiftly
10 completed together • by those in whose hearts lies the
11 desire of reaching eternal life. • Thus they take the
narrow way, as the Lord says, 'Narrow is the way that
12 leads to life.'[3] • So they do not live according to their own
wills, nor obey their own desires and pleasures, but
behaving in accordance with the rule and judgement of
another, they live in monasteries and desire to have an
13 Abbot ruling over them. • Without doubt such men
imitate the mind of the Lord in his saying, 'I came to do
not my own will, but that of him who sent me.'[4]

14 • This obedience of which we speak will be acceptable Jan. 23
May 24
Sept. 23

[1] Ps 17:44 [2] Lk 10:16 [3] Mt 7:14 [4] Jn 6:38

to God and agreeable to men if what is ordered is carried
out without fearfulness, without slowness in performance,
without half-heartedness or grumbling or an unwilling
reply. • For the obedience that is shown to superiors is 15
shown to God; for he said himself, 'He who listens to you,
listens to me.'[5] • And it should be offered by the disciples 16
with good will, because 'God loves a cheerful giver.'[6]
• For if a disciple obeys grudgingly, if he complains not 17
only in words but even in thought, • then, although he 18
carries out the order it will not now be acceptable to
God, who sees that his heart is grumbling; • and for work 19
like this he will get no reward—indeed, he incurs the
penalty for grumblers, unless he make amends with
penance.

---

[5] Lk 10:16 [6] II Co 9:7

Chapter VI On keeping silent

1 • Let us do what the prophet says, 'I have resolved: I will Jan. 24
watch how I behave and not let my tongue lead me into May 25
sin; I set a muzzle over my mouth; I stayed dumb, I was Sept. 24
humbled, I refrained from speaking even good words.'[1]
2 • Here the prophet teaches that if we should sometimes
for the sake of the virtue of silence refrain even from good
conversation, we should all the more, for fear of the
3 penalty of sin, refrain from evil words. • Therefore,
because of the great importance of keeping silence,
permission to speak should be rarely given even to
exemplary disciples, for conversation that is good and
4 holy and edifying; • for it is written, 'If you talk a lot you
5 will not escape falling into sin,'[2] • and elsewhere, 'Death
6 and life are in the power of the tongue.'[3] • Indeed it is
fitting for the master to speak and teach; the disciple's
part is to keep silent and to listen.
7 • Therefore, if it is necessary to ask a superior for
something, the request should be made with humility
8 and submissive reverence. • But as for loose talk, idle
words and talk that stimulates laughter, we condemn
this with a permanent ban in all places, and we do not
allow a disciple to open his mouth in this kind of speech.

---

[1] Ps 38:2, 3 [2] Pr 10:19 [3] Pr 18:21

Chapter VII Humility

Jan. 25 May 26 Sept. 25
• Brothers, Holy Scripture cries aloud to us, saying, 1
'Whoever exalts himself will be humbled, and he who
humbles himself will be exalted.'[1] • When it says this it is 2
teaching that all exaltation is a kind of pride. • And the 3
prophet shows that he himself was on his guard against
it, when he said, 'Lord, my heart has no lofty ambitions,
my eyes do not look too high; I am not concerned with
great affairs, or marvels beyond my scope.'[2] • Why thus? 4
'If I did not think humbly, but exalted my soul, as a child
on the mother's breast is weaned, so did you treat my
soul.'[3]

Jan. 26 May 27 Sept. 26
• So, brothers, if we wish to reach the highest peak of 5
humility, and to arrive quickly at that state of heavenly
exaltation which is attained in the present life through
humility, • then that ladder which appeared to Jacob in 6
his dream, on which he saw angels going up and down,
must be set up, so that we may mount by our own
actions. • Certainly that going down and up is to be 7
understood by us in the sense that we go down through
pride and up through humility. • The ladder itself that is 8
set up is our life in this world, and the setting up is
effected by the Lord in the humbled heart. • The sides of 9
the ladder we call the body and soul, and in them the
divine call inserts the diverse rungs of humility and
(interior) discipline.

Jan. 27 May 28 Sept. 27
• The first step of humility, then, is for a man to set the 10
fear of God always before his eyes, and utterly to avoid
forgetfulness. • He must always remember all God's 11
commandments, and constantly turn over in his heart

---

[1] Lk 18:14 [2] Ps 130:1 [3] ibid. 2

how hell will burn those who despise him by their sins,
and how eternal life has been prepared for those who fear
12 him. • At every moment a man must be on his guard
against sins and vices—vices of thought, word, hand,
foot or self-will, and also against the desires of the flesh.
13 • He must recognise that he is at every hour in the sight
of God in heaven, and that his actions are everywhere
visible to the divine eyes of God, and are being reported
14 to God by the angels from moment to moment. • This is
made clear to us by the prophet when he shows us that
God is always present in our thoughts, 'God examines',
15 he says, 'the heart and the mind.'[4] • And also, 'The Lord
16 knows exactly how men think.'[5] • And yet again, 'You
17 read my thoughts from far away'[6] • and 'Even the
18 thought of man shall praise you.'[7] • In order then to keep
his perverse thoughts under careful control, the profitable
brother should repeat in his heart, 'Then I shall be
spotless in his sight, if I keep myself in check against my
sinfulness.'[8]

19 • Scripture, indeed, forbids us to do our own will, Jan. 28
20 saying to us, 'Turn away from your will.'[9] • Moreover, May 29 Sept. 28
we ask God in our prayers that his will may be done in
21 us. • Truly then we are taught not to do our own will,
when we accept the warning of Scripture, 'There are
ways which seem right to a man, but in the end they
22 plunge him into the depth of hell,'[10] • and also when we
tremble at what is said of the indifferent, 'They are
23 corrupt and depraved in their pleasures.'[11] • Indeed in
what concerns the desires of the flesh, we must believe
that God is ever present to us, even as the prophet says,
'All my desires are known to you.'[12]

---

[4] Ps 7:10 [5] Ps 93:11 [6] Ps 138:3 [7] Ps 75:11 [8] Ps 17:24 [9] Sir 18:30 [10] Pr 16:25
[11] Ps 13:1 [12] Ps 37:10

Jan. 29 • We must, therefore, be on our guard against any evil 24
May 30
Sept. 29 desire, because death is stationed beside the entrance to
delight, • as Scripture teaches in the words, 'Do not go 25
after your lusts.'[13] • So if the eyes of the Lord are upon 26
the good and the wicked[14] • and if the Lord is always 27
looking down from heaven upon the children of men to
see if there are any that act wisely and seek after God,[15]
• and if daily our works are reported to the Lord by the 28
angels assigned to us, then brethren, • we must constantly 29
be on our guard, lest one day God beholds us falling into
sin and becoming unprofitable • and (although he spare 30
us in this life because he is merciful and waits for our
repentance) he should say to us in the hereafter, 'This
you did, and I was silent.'[16]

Jan. 30 • The second step of humility is that a man should not 31
May 31
Sept. 30 love his own will nor take pleasure in carrying out his
desires, • but rather by his actions imitate the Lord in his 32
saying, 'I came not to do my own will, but that of him
who sent me.'[17] • And it has been written, 'Self- 33
indulgence brings its penalty, endurance brings forth a
crown.'

Jan. 31 • The third step of humility is that for the love of God 34
June 1
Oct. 1 one should be obedient to a superior in all things,
imitating the Lord of whom the Apostle says, 'He was
made obedient even unto death.'[18]

Feb. 1 • The fourth step of humility is that, when in the very 35
June 2
Oct. 2 act of obeying one meets with trials, opposition, and even
abuse, a man should, with an uncomplaining spirit, keep
a firm grip on patience • and as he endures he should 36
neither grow faint nor run away; even as Scripture says,
'He who stands firm to the end will be saved,'[19] • and 37

---

[13] Sir 18:30 [14] Pr 15:3 [15] Ps 13:2 [16] Ps 49:21 [17] Jn 6:38 [18] Ph 2:8
[19] Mt 10:22

again, 'Let your heart take courage and hope in the
38 Lord.'[20] • Further, to show us how a faithful man should
suffer all things, however painful, on the Lord's behalf, it
gives voice to those who suffer in the words, 'For your
sake we are afflicted by death all the day long, and are
39 reckoned as sheep for slaughter.'[21] • Yet unmoved,
through their hope of divine reward they joyfully
persevere, saying, 'These are the trials through which
40 we triumph on account of him who has loved us.'[22] • And
elsewhere Scripture says again, 'You tested us, O God;
you refined us in the fire as silver is refined; you led us
41 into the net; you laid tribulations on our backs'[23] • And
to show that we ought to be under a superior, it
continues, 'You have set men over our heads.'[24]
42 • Precisely then they patiently fulfil the command of the
Lord in these trials and rebuffs, and when they are struck
on one cheek they offer the other.[25] When someone takes
away their tunic they allow him to take their cloak also.
43 When they are forced to go one mile, they go two; • like
the Apostle Paul they put up with false brethren, and bless
those who curse them.[26]

44 • The fifth step of humility is that a man should in Feb. 2
humble confession reveal to his Abbot all the evil June 3
thoughts that come into his mind, and any wrongful Oct. 3
45 actions that he had done in secret. • In this connection
Scripture exhorts us in the words, 'Reveal your course to
46 the Lord, and hope in him,'[27] • and again, 'Make
confession to the Lord for he is good, and his mercy is
47 everlasting;'[28] • and yet again the prophet says, 'I have
declared my sin to you, I have not covered up my evil
48 actions; • I made this resolve: I will confess my evil deeds

[20] Ps 26:14 [21] Rm 8:36 [22] ibid. 37 [23] Ps 65: 10, 11 [24] ibid. 12 [25] Mt 5:39-41
[26] I Co 4:12 [27] Ps 36:5 [28] Ps 105:1

to the Lord, and you have forgiven the guilt of my
heart.'[29]
Feb. 3 • The sixth step of humility is that a monk should be 49
June 4
Oct. 4 satisfied with whatever is of lowest value or quality, and
with regard to the tasks laid on him should think of
himself as a bad and unworthy workman, • repeating to 50
himself the words of the prophet, 'I have been brought to
nothing; I have known nothing; I am like a pack-animal
before you . . . and yet I am always with you.'[30]
Feb. 4 • The seventh step of humility is that he should not 51
June 5
Oct. 5 only say in words that he is inferior and less virtuous
than all other men, but that he should really believe it in
the depth of his heart, • making the same act of humility 52
as the prophet, who says, 'I am a worm and no man; the
scorn of mankind, the jest of the people.'[31] • 'I have been 53
lifted up, I have been brought down, and reduced to
confusion.'[32] • And again, 'It is good for me that you 54
have humiliated me, so that I may learn your commandments.'[33]
Feb. 5 • The eighth step of humility is that a monk should do 55
June 6
Oct. 6 nothing except what is recommended by the common
rule of the monastery and the example of those above
Feb. 6 him. 56
June 7
Oct. 7 •The ninth step of humility is that a monk should keep
his tongue from talking; he should preserve silence and 57
not speak until he is questioned, • for the Scripture
teaches that, 'In much talking, one will not escape sin,'[34] 58
• and that 'the talkative man is not directed in his life.'[35]
Feb. 7 • The tenth step of humility is that he should not be 59
June 8
Oct. 8 ready and quick to laughter, for it is written, 'The fool
raises his voice in laughter.'[36]

---

[29] Ps 31:5 [30] Ps 73:22, 23 [31] Ps 21:7 [32] Ps 87:16 [33] Ps 118:71 [34] Pr 10:19 [35] Ps 139:12
[36] Sir 21:23

60 • The eleventh step of humility is that when a monk Feb. 8
speaks, he does so quietly, without laughter, with June 9 Oct. 9
humility, with restraint, making use of few words and
61 reasonable ones, • as it is written, 'The wise man
becomes known for his few words.'

62 • The twelfth step of humility is not only that a monk Feb. 9
should be humble of heart, but also that in his June 10 Oct. 10
appearance his humility should be apparent to those who
see him.

63 • That is to say: whether he is at the work of God, in
the oratory, in the monastery, in the garden, on the road,
in the field or anywhere else, whether sitting, walking or
standing, he should always have his head bowed, his eyes
64 fixed on the ground, • and should at every moment be
considering his guilt for his sins and thinking that he is
65 even now being presented for the dread judgement. • He
should always be saying in his heart what the tax-
gatherer in the Gospel said with downcast eyes, 'Lord,
sinner as I am, I am not worthy to raise my eyes to
66 heaven;'[37] • or again with the prophet, 'I am bowed
down and humbled at all times.'[38]

67 • Thus when all these steps of humility have been
climbed, the monk will soon reach that love of God
68 which, being perfect, drives out all fear.[39] • Through this
love all the practices which before he kept somewhat
fearfully, he now begins to keep effortlessly and naturally
69 and habitually, • influenced now not by any fear of hell
but by the force of long practice, and the very delight he
70 experiences in virtue. • These things the Lord, working
through his Holy Spirit, will deign to show in his
workman, when he has been purified from vice and sin.

---

[37] cf. Lk 18:13 [38] Ps 118:107 [39] I Jn 4:18

Chapter VIII The Divine Office at Night

Feb. 10 • Having considered what is reasonable we lay down 1
June 11
Oct. 11 that during the winter (that is from 1 November till
Easter) the time of rising will be the eighth hour of the
night. • Thus they may sleep for a while after midnight 2
and get up after digestion has been completed. • The 3
time that is left after Matins is to be used for further
study by the brethren whose knowledge of the Psalter or
of the readings is incomplete. • From Easter till the 4
aforesaid 1 November, the hour of rising should be so
determined that there is a short interval after Matins,
during which the brethren can go out for the necessities
of nature. Lauds which follow are to be said as dawn is
breaking.

Chapter IX The Number of Psalms to be said at the Night Office

1 • During the winter period mentioned above, first of all Feb. 11
there should be said three times the versicle, 'Lord open June 12 Oct. 12
2 my lips, and my mouth will proclaim your praise,'[1] • to
3 be followed by Psalm 3 and the *Glory be*; • after this
Psalm 94 should be chanted with an antiphon, or at least
4 chanted. • Then the hymn should follow, and next, six
5 Psalms with antiphons. • When these are ended and the
versicle has been said, the Abbot should pronounce a
blessing. Then when all are seated in their stalls, three
readings should be read by the brethren in turn from the
book on the lectern, and between them three responsories
6 should be sung. • Two responsories should be sung
without the *Glory be*, but after the third reading, the
7 singer should chant the *Glory be*, • and when he begins it
all should at once rise from their seats in honour and
8 reverence for the Holy Trinity. • The books of divine
authorship, of both the Old and New Testaments, should
be read at Matins, and also the commentaries on them
written by well-known and approved Catholic Fathers.
9 • After these readings with their responsories another six
Psalms should follow; they are to be sung with Alleluia.
10 • After these Psalms, there should follow a reading from
the Apostle, recited by heart, the versicle, and the prayer
11 of the litany, that is *Lord have mercy*. • And so let Matins
conclude.

---

[1] Ps 50:17

Chapter X How the Praise of God is to be performed on Summer Nights

Feb. 12 • From Easter till November the same number of 1
June 13
Oct. 13 Psalms, as set down above, is to be retained, • but on 2
account of the nights being short, no lessons are to be
read from the book. Instead of these three readings, one
from the Old Testament is to be recited by heart,
followed by a short responsory. • All the rest should be 3
carried out as set down above. Thus, never less than
twelve Psalms should be said at Matins, not counting the
3rd and 94th.

Chapter XI How Matins are to be carried out on Sundays

1 • On Sundays the hour of rising for Matins should be Feb. 13
2 earlier. • In this Office the method is as follows. When June 14 Oct. 14
the six Psalms and the versicle have been chanted, as we
set out above, and all are seated in due order in their
stalls, four readings should be read from the book (as we
3 said before) with their responsories, • and the *Glory be* is
chanted only in the fourth responsory. When he begins it
4 all should rise at once with reverence. • After these
readings another six Psalms should follow in order with
5 antiphons, as before, and a versicle. • After these again
four more lessons should be read with responsories, as set
6 out before. • Then three canticles from the prophets, as
chosen by the Abbot, should be sung with Alleluia.
7 • When the verse has been said, the Abbot gives a
blessing, and four more lessons are read from the New
8 Testament in the way already described. • After the
fourth responsory the Abbot intones the hymn *We praise*
9 *you, O God;* • when this is finished the Abbot reads from
10 the Gospel, while all stand in reverential honour. • At
the end of the reading all reply *Amen*, and then the Abbot
begins the hymn *To You Praise is due*, and after the prayer,
11 they begin Lauds. • This order of Matins is to be kept on
12 Sundays in both the summer and winter seasons— •
unless by chance they get up late (which should not
happen) and some abridgement of the readings or
13 responsories has to be made. • But great care should be
taken that this does not happen, but if it does, the person
through whose carelessness it has occurred must make
adequate satisfaction to God in the oratory.

Chapter XII How the Solemn Office of Lauds is to be carried out

Feb. 14 June 15 Oct. 15
• Lauds on Sunday begin with Psalm 66, chanted 1
continuously without an antiphon. • After that, Psalm 50 2
is chanted with Alleluia. • And then Psalm 117 and 3
Psalm 62. • Then the canticle *O All you Works of the Lord,* 4
Bless the Lord, and the *Praises*,[1] a reading from the
Apocalypse learnt by heart, a responsory, the hymn, the
versicle, the canticle from the Gospels, and the litany to
form the conclusion.

[1] Psalms 148-50

Chapter XIII How Lauds are carried out on ordinary Days

1 • On ordinary days the solemn Office of Lauds is to be Feb. 15
2 carried out as follows: • Psalm 66 is to be said without an June 16 Oct. 16
antiphon, and rather slowly (as on Sunday) so that all
may arrive in time for Psalm 50 which is to be chanted
3 with an antiphon. • After this, let two more Psalms be
4 chanted, keeping to custom, namely: • on Monday 5 and
5, 6 35, • on Tuesday 42 and 56, • on Wednesday 63 and 64,
7, 8, 9 • on Thursday 87 and 89, • on Friday 75 and 91, • and
on Saturday 142, and the canticle of Deuteronomy,
10 divided into two parts. • On each of the other days is
sung a canticle from the prophets, as in the Roman
11 Church. • The *Praises* follow, and then a single reading
from the Apostle to be recited by heart, the responsory,
hymn, verse, canticle from the Gospels, and the litany to
form the end.

12 • Definitely neither Lauds nor Vespers should finish Feb. 16
without the Lord's Prayer being recited at the end by the June 17 Oct. 17
superior, while all listen. This is on account of the thorns
of mutual offence which occur in the course of events;
13 • for in this way they are warned by the undertaking
contained in the words of the prayer, *Forgive us as we
forgive* and may cleanse their hearts from any defect of
14 this kind. • In the other Offices only the last part of this
prayer is said, so that all may reply, *But deliver us from evil.*

Chapter XIV How Matins are carried out on Feast Days of Saints

Feb. 17 June 18 Oct. 18

• On the feasts of saints and on all solemn days Matins 1
are to be carried out as we have laid down for Sundays,
• except that the Psalms, antiphons and readings proper 2
to the day should be said; but the order of the Office
should be as previously detailed.

Chapter XV When Alleluia is to be said

1 • From the holy feast of Easter until Pentecost Alleluia should be said throughout the Office both in the Psalms and in the responses. Feb. 18 June 19 Oct. 19

2 • From Pentecost till the beginning of Lent it should be said every night with the second group of Psalms only.

3 • On every Sunday (outside Lent) the canticles of Matins, Lauds, Prime, Terce, Sext and None should be said with Alleluia; but Vespers should be sung with an antiphon.

4 • Except from Easter to Pentecost, responsories are never to be said with Alleluia.

Chapter XVI How the Work of God is carried out during the Daytime

Feb. 19
June 20
Oct. 20

• As the prophet puts it, 'Seven times daily I have 1
praised you.'[1] • This sacred number of seven will be 2
performed by us if we carry out the duties of our service
at Lauds, Prime, Terce, Sext, None, Vespers and
Compline, • for it is of these hours of the day that he said, 3
'Seven times a day I have praised you.' • And of the 4
Night Office the same prophet said, 'At midnight I got
up to give you praise.'[2] • Let us therefore at these times 5
give praise to our Creator 'for his righteous judgements',[3]
that is to say at Lauds, Prime, Terce, Sext, None,
Vespers and Compline, and at night let us get up to
praise him.

---

[1] Ps 118:164 [2] ibid:62 [3] ibid:164

Chapter XVII How many Psalms are to be said at these Hours

1 • The order of the Psalmody at Matins and Lauds has already been dealt with; now we must consider the Feb. 20 June 21 Oct. 21
2 remaining hours. • At Prime three Psalms should be
3 said, separately, and not under one *Glory be*. • The hymn is sung after the versicle, *O God come to my aid,*[1] before
4 beginning the Psalms. • When the three Psalms are finished there should be one lesson, a versicle, *Lord have*
5 *mercy* and the concluding prayers. • The Offices of Terce, Sext and None are to be carried out in the same way, thus: the opening verse, the hymn of the hour, the three Psalms, a reading and verse, *Lord have mercy* and the
6 concluding prayers. • If the community is large enough antiphons should be used; otherwise the Psalms are sung straight through.

7 • For the evening prayer meeting four Psalms with
8 antiphons will be enough. • After them a lesson should be recited, then a responsory, a hymn, a versicle, a canticle from the Gospels, the litany and the Lord's prayer at the end.

9 • For Compline the recitation of three Psalms, said
10 straight through without an antiphon, is enough. • After these there will be the hymn proper to this hour, a lesson, a versicle, *Lord have mercy*, and the blessing at the end.

---

[1] Ps 69:1

Chapter XVIII In what order the Psalms should be said

Feb. 21 • First should be said the verse, *O God come to my aid, Lord* 1
June 22 *make haste to help me,* and *Glory be*; then the hymn of the
Oct. 22 hour.
• Then at Prime on Sunday are to be said four stanzas 2
of Psalm 118; • at the remaining hours, namely Terce, 3
Sext and None, three stanzas of the same Psalm are to be
said.
• At Prime on Monday three Psalms, namely 1, 2 and 4
6 are to be said, • and so on each day at Prime up to 5
Psalm 19, continuing till Sunday (exclusively); but note
that Psalms 9 and 17 are to be divided into two parts.
• In this way the Sunday Matins will always begin with 6
Psalm 20.
Feb. 22 • At Terce, Sext and None on Mondays are to be said 7
June 23 the nine remaining stanzas of Psalm 118, three at each
Oct. 23 hour. • Psalm 118 is thus finished on two days, Sunday 8
and Monday; • on Tuesday three Psalms are to be 9
chanted at each of Terce, Sext and None, from 119 to
127, nine Psalms in all. • And these Psalms are to be 10
repeated daily at the same hours until Sunday; but the
arrangement of hymns, readings and verses is to follow
the same pattern daily, • and on Sunday a new 11
beginning should be made with Psalm 118.
Feb. 23 • Vespers are to be sung each day with four Psalms, 12
June 24 • beginning with Psalm 109 and ending with Psalm 147, 13
Oct. 24 • but excluding those which are assigned to other hours, 14
namely Psalms 117–27, 133 and 142; • the rest are all to 15
be said at Vespers. • Since, however, there are three 16
Psalms too few, the longer Psalms of those just

mentioned, namely 138, 143, 144 are to be divided into
17 two. • On the other hand Psalm 116, being very short, is
to be joined with 115.
18 • This covers the order of the Psalms for Vespers: all
the other items, namely the reading, responsory, hymn,
versicle and canticle, are to be performed as we have laid
19 down above. • At Compline the same Psalms are to be
repeated daily, namely 4, 90 and 133.
20 • This settles the order of the Psalms during the day: Feb. 24 (in L. Yr.) June 25 Oct. 25
all the remaining Psalms are to be divided equally into
the seven vigils of the night: twelve are to be allotted to
21 each night, • but dividing the Psalms of greater length.
22 • Nevertheless, we emphasise that if anyone is dis-
satisfied with this arrangement of the Psalms, he is to
23 organise them otherwise as he finds better; • he should,
however, see to it that the Psalter be recited every week,
24 starting anew from vigils of the Lord's Day. • For monks
who in the course of a week sing less than the Psalter
with its usual canticles manifest a service too slothful for
25 their dedicated state, • since we read that our holy
Fathers vigorously completed in a single day what it is to
be hoped we who are tepid may accomplish in a whole
week.

Chapter XIX Recollection in chanting

Feb. 24 (or 25) June 26 Oct. 26

• We believe that God is present everywhere, and that 1
the eyes of the Lord are in every place, keeping watch on
the good and the bad;[1] • but most of all should we 2
believe this without any shadow of doubt, when we are
engaged in the work of God. • We should therefore 3
always be mindful of the prophet's words, 'Serve the
Lord with fear.'[2] • And again, 'Sing wisely.'[3] • And yet 4, 5
again, 'In the sight of the angels I will sing to you.'[4] • We 6
must therefore consider how we should behave in the
sight of the Divine Majesty and his Angels, • and as we 7
sing our Psalms let us see to it that our mind is in
harmony with our voice.

---

[1] Pr 15:3 [2] Ps 2:11 [3] Ps 46:8 [4] Ps 137:2

Chapter XX Reverence at Prayer

1 • If we wish to bring anything to the attention of Feb. 25
powerful men, it is only with humility and reverence that (or 26) June 27
2 we dare to do so. • How much more then should we Oct. 27
present our supplications to the Lord God of all things
with complete humility and devout purity of mind.
3 • Indeed we must grasp that it is not by using many
words[1] that we shall get our prayers answered, but by
4 purity of heart and repentance with tears. • Prayer,
therefore, should be short and pure, unless on occasion it
be drawn out by the feeling of the inspiration of divine
5 grace. • In community, however, the prayer should be
kept quite short, and when the superior gives the sign all
should rise together.

---

[1] Mt 6:7

Chapter XXI Of the Deans of the Monastery

Feb. 26 (or 27) June 28 Oct. 28

• If the community is rather large, brethren of good 1
reputation and holy way of life should be selected from
among them and appointed deans. • They are to exercise 2
care over their deaneries in all respect according to the
commandments of God and the instructions of their
Abbot. • They should be chosen as deans who are such 3
that the Abbot may be able to share his burdens with
them with confidence. • They should not be chosen 4
according to seniority but for their merits and their
wisdom in teaching. • And if any of these deans, 5
becoming inflated with some form of pride, be found
worthy of rebuke, he is to be corrected once, twice,
indeed three times; but if he will not amend, he should be
removed • and another who is worthy should be 6
substituted for him. • And we lay down the same 7
procedure for the Prior of the Monastery.

Chapter XXII How the Monks should sleep

1, 2 • The brethren are to sleep each in a single bed. • These Feb. 27
beds are assigned to them in order according to the (or 28)
length of their monastic life, subject to the Abbot's June 29 Oct. 29
3 discretion. • If it is possible, all should sleep in one place,
but if their numbers do not permit this, they should take
their rest by tens or twenties with the seniors who are
4 entrusted with their care. • A candle should burn
5 continuously in this room till morning. • They should
sleep clothed, girt with girdles or cords, but not with
their knives at their sides as they sleep, for fear that a
6 brother should be wounded while asleep. • And so let the
monks be always ready, and when the signal is given,
they should get up without delay and make haste to
arrive first for the Work of God, but in a gentle and
7 orderly way. • The younger brethren should not have
their beds together, but dispersed among the seniors.
8 • When they get up for the Work of God they may
quietly encourage one another since the sleepy are given
to making excuses.

Chapter XXIII Excommunication for Faults

Feb. 28 (or 29) June 30 Oct. 30

• If any brother is found to be contumacious or 1
disobedient or arrogant or a grumbler or one who sets
himself up against some point of the Holy Rule or
despises the ordinances of his seniors, • he is to be 2
warned privately once or twice, according to our Lord's
command,[1] by his superiors. • If he does not amend his 3
ways, then he should be publicly rebuked before all. • If 4
he still does not improve let him undergo excommunication, if he understands the nature of this punishment.
• If, however, he is stubborn, he must undergo corporal 5
punishment.

---

[1] Mt 18:15-16

Chapter XXIV How Excommunication is to be regulated

1 • Excommunication or disciplinary measures should be Mar. 1
2 proportionate to the nature of the fault, • and the nature July 1 Oct. 31
3 of faults is for the Abbot to judge. • If then a brother is
found to commit less serious faults he is to be deprived of
4 sharing in the common meal. • The rules for one who is
thus excluded from the sharing in the common meal will
be: he may not intone antiphon or Psalm in the oratory;
nor may he read a lesson until he has made satisfaction.
5 • He must eat alone after the meal of the brethren.
6 • Thus if they eat at the sixth hour, he will eat in the
7 evening; • until having made adequate satisfaction he
receives pardon.

Chapter XXV Very serious Faults

Mar. 2 July 2 Nov. 1

• The brother who is guilty of a very serious fault is to be 1
suspended from sharing in the meals and also from the
oratory. • None of the brethren may associate with him 2
in companionship or conversation. • He is to be left alone 3
at the work assigned to him and to remain in penitent
grief as he reflects on the terrible sentence of the Apostle.
• 'This kind of man is handed over to bodily death, so 4
that his spirit may be saved for the day of the Lord.'[1]
• His food he should take alone in such measure and at 5
such time as the Abbot thinks most suitable for him;
• nor may he or the food that is given him receive a 6
blessing from anyone who passes by.

[1] I Co 5:5

Chapter XXVI Unauthorised Association with the Excommunicated

1 • If any brother, acting without instructions from the Abbot, takes it upon himself to associate with an excommunicated brother in any way, or to talk with him, Mar. 3 July 3 Nov. 2
2 or send him a message, • he must likewise undergo the punishment of excommunication.

Chapter XXVII The Concern the Abbot must have for the Excommunicated

Mar. 4 July 4 Nov. 3

• The Abbot should carry out with the deepest concern 1
his responsibility for the brethren who fall into sin, ‘for it
is not those who are in good health who need a doctor,
but those who are sick.’[1] • For this reason he should, like 2
a skilful doctor, use every possible remedy; for example
he may send *senpectae* (that is, mature and wise brethren)
• to give unofficial consolation to their wavering brother, 3
and induce him to make humble satisfaction, and give
him comfort, ‘so that he is not overcome by too much
sadness.’[2] • And so let it be as the Apostle also says, ‘that 4
love is reaffirmed towards him’;[3] and everybody is to
pray for him.

• It is indeed very important that the Abbot should 5
show his concern, and make speed to employ his skill and
energy, lest he lose one of the sheep entrusted to him.
• For he must bear in mind that it is the care of sick souls 6
that he has undertaken, not a despotic rule over healthy
ones. • Moreover, he should fear the threats of the 7
prophet, through whose words God says, ‘What you saw
to be fat you took, and what was weak you threw away.’[4]
• And let him copy the loving example of the Good 8
Shepherd who left the ninety-nine sheep on the mountains, and went away to search for the one that had gone
astray; • and had such pity for its weakness that he 9
deigned to lay it on his own sacred shoulders, and so
carry it back to the flock.[5]

[1] Mt 9:12 [2] II Co 2:7 [3] ibid:8 [4] Ezk 34:3, 4 [5] Lk 15:4, 5

Chapter XXVIII The Incorrigible

1 • If any brother who has been often corrected for some Mar. 5
fault, and even been excommunicated, does not amend July 5 Nov. 4
his way, he must receive harsher punishment, that is to
2 say, he must suffer a beating. • But if, even after this, he
does not amend or if—which God forbid—he is so filled
with pride as to want to defend his actions, then the
3 Abbot must act like a wise doctor. • If he has made use of
poultices, of the ointments of his counsels, of the
remedies of Divine Scripture, if he has come at last to the
cautery of excommunication, and the blows of the rod,
4 • and if he now sees that his work is unavailing—let him
make use of what is still greater: his own prayer
5 combined with that of all the brethren • that the Lord to
whom nothing is impossible may work the salvation of
the sick brother.

6 • But if even by this means he is not cured then the
Abbot must employ the surgeon's knife, as the Apostle
says, 'Drive out the wicked man from among you.'[1]
7 • And again, 'If the unfaithful one leaves you, let him
8 go,'[2] • for fear that one diseased sheep may infect the
whole flock.

---

[1] Co 5:13 [2] I Co 7:15

Chapter XXIX Whether Brethren who leave should be taken back

Mar. 6 • If a brother has through his own wrong choice left the 1
July 6 monastery and wants to come back again, he must first
Nov. 5 promise to make amendment for having left, • and then 2
let him be taken back in the lowest place as a test of his
humility. • If he goes away a second time, he may be 3
received back, and even a third time; but after that he
must realise that the path of return will not be granted
him again.

Chapter XXX How Boys are to be corrected

1 • Disciplinary measures should be appropriate to every Mar. 7
2 age and intelligence: • hence when boys or youths or July 7 Nov. 6
others, incapable of understanding how serious a
3 punishment excommunication is, • commit offences,
such persons are to suffer additional fasts or painful
stripes, so that they may be cured.

2
The Administration of the Monastery

Chapter XXXI What Kind of Man the Cellarer of the Monastery should be

1 • As cellarer of the monastery should be chosen from the Mar. 8
community one who is sound in judgement, mature in July 8 Nov. 7
character, sober, not a great eater, not self-important,
not turbulent, not harshly spoken, not an off-putter, not
2 wasteful, • but a God-fearing man who will be a father to
3 the whole community. • He is to have charge of all
4 affairs, • but he is not to act without the Abbot's
5,6 approval, • and he must carry out his orders. • He must
7 not sadden the brethren. • If any brother happens to
make an unreasonable demand of him, he should not
upset him by showing contempt, but refuse the ill-
8 advised petitioner with reasons modestly presented. • He
must keep guard over his own soul, always bearing in
mind that saying of the Apostle that he who has
ministers well gains a good reputation for himself.[1]
9 • With all compassion he is to have care for the sick, the
children, the guests and the poor, knowing for certain
that in the day of judgement he will have to render
10 account for his treatment of them all. • He must regard
the chattels of the monastery and its whole property as if
11 they were the sacred vessels of the altar. • He should
12 neglect nothing. • He must neither succumb to avarice
nor be a wasteful squanderer of the monastery's goods;
but he should conduct all his affairs with prudence and
in accordance with the Abbot's instructions.

13 • It is essential that he should have humility and if he Mar. 9
has nothing material to give, he should at least offer a July 9 Nov. 8
14 kind word of reply, • as it is written, 'A good word

[1] I Tm 3:13

surpasses the best gift.'[2] • He must keep under his own 15
care whatever the Abbot has entrusted to him, but he
should not undertake anything the Abbot has forbidden.
• He must provide the brethren with their regular 16
allowance of food, without fuss or keeping them waiting,
so as not to make for them an occasion of sin, keeping in
mind the divine saying about the retribution of him 'who
causes one of the little ones to sin.'[3] • If the community is 17
rather large, helpers should be given him, so that with
their aid he may himself tranquilly perform the office
entrusted to him.

• Whatever has to be asked for or given should be 18
asked for or given at suitable times, • so that no one may 19
be upset or saddened in the household of God.

---

[2] Sir 18:17 [3] Mt 18:6

Chapter XXXII The Tools and Goods of the Monastery

1 • With regard to the monastery's material possessions Mar. 10
such as tools, clothes, or other articles, the Abbot should July 10 Nov. 9
put in charge of them brethren whose way of life and
2 character he can trust, • and then commit all these
things to them, as he thinks best, for safe keeping, and
3 return after use. • The Abbot should keep a list of them
so that when the brethren succeed one another in the
tasks assigned to them he may know what is being
4 handed over or received back. • If anyone treats the
property of the monastery in a dirty or careless manner,
5 he should be corrected • and if he does not amend, he
should suffer punishment as laid down in the Rule.

Chapter XXXIII Whether Monks may have personal Property

Mar. 11 • It is of the greatest importance that this vice should be 1
July 11
Nov. 10 totally eradicated from the monastery. • No one may 2
take it upon himself to give or receive anything without
the Abbot's permission • or to possess anything as his 3
own, anything whatever, books or writing tablets or pen
or anything at all; • for they are not allowed to retain at 4
their own disposition their own bodies or wills, • but they 5
must expect to receive all they need from the Father of
the monastery. And so it must not be allowed that
anyone should have anything which the Abbot has not
approved. • Everything should be common to all, as it is 6
written, and no one should call anything his own[1] or
treat it as such. • But if anyone is found to be 7
entertaining this wicked vice, he should be warned once,
and a second time; if he does not amend, he should
undergo punishment.

[1] Ac 4:32

Chapter XXXIV Whether all should receive equal Shares

1 • It is written, 'Distribution was made to each as he had Mar. 12
2 need.'[1] • By this we do not say that favouritism should be July 12 Nov. 11
shown to persons, far from it, but that infirmities should
3 be allowed for. • If someone needs less he should thank
4 God and not be upset; • if another needs more he should
be humble about his weakness, and not feel important on
5 account of the consideration shown him, • and thus all
6 members will be at peace. • Above all the bad habit of
grumbling must not make its appearance in any word or
7 gesture for any reason whatever. • If anyone is found
guilty of this, let him pay a heavy penalty.

[1] Ac 4:35

Chapter XXXV The weekly Servers in the Kitchen

Mar. 13 • The brethren should serve one another, and no one 1
July 13
Nov. 12 should be excused from kitchen duty except for sickness
or because he is more usefully engaged elsewhere,
• because through this service the reward of an increase 2
in charity is gained. • For the weak, however, help 3
should be provided so that this duty may not cause them
dejection. • Indeed all should have help according to the 4
size of the community and the location. • If the 5
community is rather large the cellarer should be excused
from kitchen duty and, as we said before, also those who
are engaged in more important tasks. • The test should 6
serve one another in turn with charity. • The one who is 7
finishing his week's duty does the washing on the
Saturday; • he should also wash the towels with which 8
the brethren dry their hands and feet. • Moreover, he 9
who is ending his week's service together with him who is
about to start should wash the feet of all.[1] • The outgoing 10
server must restore the crockery he has made use of,
washed and intact to the cellarer, • and the cellarer must 11
hand it over to the incomer, so that he knows what he is
giving out and what he is getting back.

May 14 • An hour before the meal, the weekly servers may 12
July 14
Nov. 13 each receive, in addition to the allotted quantity, a drink
and some bread, • so that at the hour of the meal they 13
may serve their brethren without finding the work heavy
or complaining. • On solemn days, however, they must 14
wait for the Mass. • On Sundays, immediately after 15
Lauds, the incoming and outgoing servers should
prostrate themselves at the feet of all the brethren in the

[1] cf. Jn 13:15

16 oratory, and ask to be prayed for. • The outgoing server
is to say the verse, 'Blessed are you Lord God for you
17 have helped and strengthened me.'[2] • When this has
been said three times, and he has received a blessing, the
incoming server follows and says, 'O God come to my
18 aid, Lord make haste to help me.'[3] • And this too is to be
repeated three times by all. And so, having received the
blessing, he begins his week's duty.

---

[2] Dn 3:28 combined with Ps 85:17 [3] Ps 69:1

Chapter XXXVI Sick Brethren

Mar. 15 • The care of the sick is to be given priority over 1
July 15
Nov. 14 everything else, so that they are indeed served as Christ
would be served, • since he said of himself, 'I was sick 2
and you visited me,'[1] • and 'What you did to one of the 3
least, you did to me.'[2] • But the sick themselves must 4
realise that it is to pay honour to God that they are being
served, and they must not vex their brethren by asking
for too much. • However, they must be borne with 5
patience, because through them a very ample recompense
is merited. • Therefore let the Abbot pay the greatest 6
attention so that they suffer no neglect.

• For the sick brethren a separate room must be 7
provided, and to serve them a brother who is God-
fearing, diligent and zealous. • The use of baths should 8
be allowed to the sick as often as is desirable, but to the
healthy and the young this should not be granted very
often. • Moreover, the eating of meat should be allowed 9
to the sick who are in a weak condition, but when they
are restored to health again, all should abstain from
meat as usual. • The Abbot must take the greatest care 10
that the sick are not neglected by the cellarer or those
who serve them, for whatever is done wrong by his
disciples concerns him.

[1] Mt 25:36 [2] ibid: 40

Chapter XXXVII Old Men and Children

1 • Although human nature itself is drawn to feel sympathy Mar. 16
for those in these stages of life, namely the old and July 16
children, yet it is right that the authority of the Rule also Nov. 15
2 should have regard to them. • Their weaknesses should
at all times be taken into consideration, and the letter of
the Rule should by no means be applied to them in
3 matters of food. • Indeed they should always be thought
of compassionately, and they should have their meals
before the prescribed times.

Chapter XXXVIII The weekly Reader

Mar. 17 July 17 Nov. 16 • At the meals of the brethren there should always be 1
reading, but not by anyone who happens to take up the
book. There shall be a reader for the whole week, and he
is to begin on Sunday. • Let him begin after Mass and 2
Communion by asking the prayers of all that God may
keep from him the spirit of vanity. • The reader himself 3
is to intone the verse, *O Lord open my lips, and my mouth shall*
proclaim your praise,[1] and it is to be said three times by all.
• And so, having received a blessing, let him begin to 4
read. • There is to be complete silence, so that no 5
whisper nor any voice other than that of the reader be
heard there. • Whatever is wanted for eating and 6
drinking the brethren should pass to one another, so that
no one need ask for anything. • If, however, something is 7
wanted, it should be asked for by some sign or sound
rather than by speaking. • No one there present is to ask 8
any question about the reading or about anything, so
that no opportunity for disturbance may arise; • unless 9
perhaps the superior wishes to say a few words for
edification. • The weekly reader may take some refresh- 10
ment before he begins to read because of his Holy
Communion and lest his fast should be a burden to him.
• He is to take his meal afterwards with the weekly cooks 11
and servers.

• The brethren are not to read (or sing) in their order 12
of seniority but only those who edify the listeners.

[1] Ps 50:17

Chapter XXXIX The Measure of Food

1 • We consider it to be enough for the daily meal, whether Mar. 18
at the sixth or the ninth hour, that there should always July 18 Nov. 17
be served two cooked dishes, to allow for the weaknesses
2 of different eaters; • so that if someone cannot eat of the
3 one dish he may still make a meal from the other. • So
two cooked dishes should be enough for all the brethren.
And if fruit or tender vegetables are to be had, a third
4 dish may be added. • A full pound of bread should be
enough for a day, whether there is one meal or those of
5 dinner and supper. • If there is a supper a third of the
pound of bread should be kept back by the cellarer and
produced at that meal.

6 • If, however, their work is rather heavy, it will be in
the Abbot's power and in his judgement to decide
7 whether it is expedient to increase the allowance. • But
there must be no danger of over-eating, so that no monk
8 is overtaken by indigestion, • for there is nothing so opp-
9 osed to Christian life as over-eating, • as our Lord says,
'Take care that your hearts are not weighed down by
10 over-eating.'[1] • Young boys should not be given the same
amount of food, but less than their elders. Frugality
11 should be the rule on all occasions. • All must refrain
entirely from eating the flesh of quadrupeds, except for
the sick who are really weak.

[1] Lk 21:34

Chapter XL The Measure of Drink

Mar. 19 • 'Each man has his special gift from God, one of one 1
July 19
Nov. 18 kind, another of another kind,'[1] • and hence it is with 2
some diffidence that we fix the quantity of the food and
drink of others. • But keeping in view the frailty of the 3
weak, we think that half a pint of wine daily is enough for
each. • Those, however, to whom God grants the 4
capacity to abstain should know that they will have their
own reward.

• If, however, local conditions or their work or the 5
summer heat call for more, it must be for the superior to
decide, but he must take care that neither excess nor
drunkenness overtakes them. • For although we read 6
that wine is not at all a drink for monks, yet, since in our
days it is impossible to persuade monks of this, let us
agree at least about this that we should not drink our fill,
but more sparingly, • since 'wine leads even wise men 7
into infidelity.'[2]

• When, however, local conditions bring it about that 8
the above mentioned quantity is not available, but much
less, or none at all, then those who live there should bless
God and not grumble. • We lay special stress on this that 9
the brethren remain free from grumbling.

---

[1] I Co 7:7 [2] Sir 19:2

Chapter XLI At what Hours they should take their Meals

1 • From the holy feast of Easter until Pentecost the Mar. 20
brethren are to have their dinner at midday, and their July 20 Nov. 19
2 supper in the evening. • From Pentecost throughout the
summer, unless the monks have work in the fields or the
summer is oppressively hot, they should fast on Wednes-
3 days and Fridays until the ninth hour, • and on the other
4 days have dinner at midday; • but the midday meal may
be kept up continuously throughout the week, if they
have work in the fields or the summer heat is excessive; it
5 will be for the Abbot to decide. • For he is to modify and
organise all their affairs in such wise that their souls may
be saved, and that the brethren do whatever they do,
without justification for grumbling.

6 • From 14 September, however, until the beginning of Lent they should always have their meal at the ninth hour.

7 • During Lent until Easter it should be in the evening.

8 • Vespers, however, should be sung at such an hour
that the brethren will not need lamp-light for their meal,
9 but that everything will be finished by daylight. • Indeed
at all seasons, the hour of supper or of the evening meal
should be calculated so that everything may be done by
daylight.

Chapter XLII That no one may speak after Compline

Mar. 21 • At all times monks ought to strive to keep silence but 1
July 21
Nov. 20 particularly so during the hours of the night, • and this 2
means in all seasons, whether on days of fasting or on
days of having a midday meal.

• If it is the latter season, then after rising from supper, 3
they should at once sit together and one of them should
read the *Conferences* or the *Lives of the Fathers* or some
other work which will edify the hearers, • but not the 4
Heptateuch or the Books of Kings; for this part of
Scripture will not be helpful to those of weaker
intelligence at this hour; they should, however, be read at
some other time.

• If it has been a fast day, then after Vespers there will 5
be a short interval, and then they should assemble for the
reading of the *Conferences* as we have said. • Four or five 6
pages should be read, or as many as the time permits;
• and during this space of time for reading all come 7
together, including anyone who may have been occupied
in a job assigned to him.

• So when all are assembled, they should say 8
Compline, and when they come out of Compline there
should be no further permission for anyone to talk about
anything. • If anyone is found transgressing this rule of 9
silence he is to be punished severely, • unless the need to 10
attend to guests has arisen, or it happens that the Abbot
has given someone an order. • And in this case, too, the 11
matter is to be handled with all seriousness and genuine
moderation.

Chapter XLIII Latecomers to the Work of God or to Meals

1 • As soon as the signal for the Divine Office is heard, the Mar. 22
brethren must leave whatever they have been engaged in July 22 Nov. 21
2 doing, and hasten with all speed; • but with dignity, so
3 that foolishness finds no stimulus. • Nothing, therefore,
is to be given preference over the Work of God.

4 • If at the Night Office anyone arrives after the *Glory
be* of Psalm 94, which for this reason we wish to be said
altogether slowly and deliberately, he must not stand in
5 his place in the choir, • but last of all, or in a place set
apart by the Abbot for such careless persons, so that they
6 may be seen by the Abbot and by everyone else, • until at
the end of the Work of God he does penance by public
7 satisfaction. • We have thought it best that such persons
should stand last or else apart, so that being shamed
because they are noticed by everybody, they may for this
8 motive mend their ways. • For if they stay outside the
oratory, there may be someone who will go back and go
to sleep again, or maybe sit down outside the oratory and
give himself up to gossip, and in this way an opportunity
9 is given to the evil one; • it is better that they go in and
not lose the benefit of the whole Office: and they should
mend their ways as well.

10 • At the Day Hours anyone who has not arrived at the
Work of God after the versicle and the *Glory be* of the first
Psalm that follows it, must take the last place as we have
11 laid down above, • nor may he take for granted
permission to join the choir as they sing, until he has
made satisfaction, unless the Abbot pardons him and
12 gives him permission; • nevertheless one guilty of this

fault should still make satisfaction.
Mar. 23 July 23 Nov. 22 • With regard to meals, the brother who does not 13
arrive before the verse, so that all may say the verse and
pray together and go to their meal together, • that is the 14
brother who does not arrive either through carelessness
or other fault, should be admonished twice for this
behaviour. • If then he does not amend, he will not be 15
permitted to share the common meal, • but will be 16
separated from the companionship of the others to eat
alone, and will be deprived of his portion of wine, until
he makes satisfaction and improves. • The same applies 17
to anyone who absents himself from the verse said after
the meal.

• Moreover, no one should be so bold as to take any 18
food or drink before or after the regular meal time. • But 19
if something is offered to a brother by the superior and he
rejects it, then when he does want what he previously
rejected, or something else, he is not to receive anything
at all until he makes suitable satisfaction.

Chapter XLIV How the Excommunicated are to make Satisfaction

1 • If, for serious faults, anyone is excommunicated from the oratory and from the common meals, he is to lie prostrate at the threshold of the oratory at the time when the Work of God is being carried out, saying nothing, Mar. 24 July 24 Nov. 23
2 • but just lying there with his head to the ground at the
3 feet of them all as they come out of the oratory. • This he is to continue to do until the Abbot considers the
4 satisfaction to be enough. • When at the Abbot's bidding he comes in, he must cast himself at the feet of the Abbot and then at the feet of the others, that they may pray for
5 him. • Then following the Abbot's instructions he may be admitted into choir, in such position as the Abbot
6 decides, • but on condition that he does not presume to sing alone any Psalm or reading or anything else, until
7 the Abbot gives a fresh order. • Moreover, at every hour, when the Work of God is being finished, he is to cast himself on the ground in the place where he is standing.
8 • And so must continue to do penance, until the Abbot again orders him to stop making this satisfaction.

9 • With regard to those who for less serious faults are excommunicated from meals only, they are to make satisfaction in the oratory until the Abbot orders them to
10 stop. • They perform this penance until the Abbot gives his blessing and says, 'That is enough.'

Chapter XLV Those who make Mistakes in the Oratory

Mar. 25 • If anyone goes wrong in giving out a Psalm, responsory, 1
July 25
Nov. 24 antiphon or reading, unless by making satisfaction he
humbles himself there before all, he must submit to
greater punishment; • for he refused to put right with 2
humility what he did wrong through lack of care. • And 3
boys should be beaten for such a fault.

Chapter XLVI Those who commit Faults in other Matters

1 • If anyone while engaged in his work, in the kitchen, in Mar. 26
the cellarer's offices, in the storeroom, in the bakery, in July 26 Nov. 25
the garden or while engaged in any craft, or indeed
2 anywhere else, behaves badly • or breaks some article or
3 destroys it, or commits some excess, • he should come
straightaway before the Abbot and the community,
declare his transgression and make satisfaction. But if he
4 does not do this, • and the transgression becomes known
through another, he must undergo a heavier penalty.

5 • However, if the failing be an interior sin, he should
6 declare it only to the Abbot or to spiritual fathers, • for
they, knowing how to heal their own wounds, know how
to heal those of others, without revealing them or making
them known.

Chapter XLVII The Signal for the Work of God

Mar. 27 • To give the signal for the Work of God, whether by day 1
July 27
Nov. 26 or by night, is the responsibility of the Abbot. He may do
it himself or he may lay the charge on a brother
sufficiently responsible to ensure that everything is
performed at the correct time. • The intoning of Psalms 2
and antiphons is to be done in turn after the Abbot by
those appointed. • No one should venture to sing or read 3
unless he can do it to the edification of his hearers • It is 4
to be done with humility, gravity and reverence, and by
appointment of the Abbot.

Chapter XLVIII The daily manual Labour

1 • Idleness is the enemy of the soul. For this reason the Mar. 28 July 28
brethren should be occupied at certain times in manual Nov. 27
2 labour, and at other times in sacred reading. • Hence we
think that the times for these two duties may be arranged
as follows:
3 • From Easter till 14 September, they should be set out
in the morning and work at whatever is necessary from
4 the first hour till about the fourth. • From the fourth
hour until about the sixth, they should be engaged in
5 reading. • After the sixth hour, and when they have had
their meal, they may rest on their beds in complete
silence, or if anyone has a mind to read, he may do so,
6 but in such a way as not to disturb anyone else. • None
should be said rather early, at about the middle of the
eighth hour, and then they should work again at
7 whatever their tasks are until Vespers. • If, however,
local necessity or their own poverty compels them to
work personally at gathering the harvest, they should not
8 be upset about this. • For then truly are they monks, if
they live by the work of their hands, as did our Fathers
9 and the Apostles. • All their labours, however, should be
kept under control on account of the less courageous.
10 • From 14 September until the beginning of Lent they Mar. 29 July 29
should be free for reading till the end of the second hour. Nov. 28
11 • Then Terce should be said, and all should work at their
12 allotted tasks until None. • At the first signal for None
every brother should detach himself from his work, so as
13 to be ready for the sounding of the second signal. • After
their evening meal they should give themselves to
reading or to studying the Psalms.

• In Lent, however, the hours for reading are from the 14
morning until the end of the third hour. Then until the
end of the tenth hour they should work at their allotted
tasks.
• And during these days of Lent everyone should receive 15
a book from the library, which he should read through
from the beginning. • These books are to be given out at 16
the beginning of Lent. • It is important that one or two 17
seniors should be appointed to go round the monastery
during the hours when the brethren are engaged in
reading, • to see whether perchance they come upon 18
some lazy brother who is engaged in doing nothing or in
chatter, and is not intent upon his book, and so not only
profitless to himself but leading others astray. • If such a 19
one is found (which we hope will not be the case) he
should be reprimanded once and a second time • and if 20
he does not amend, he should be punished in accordance
with the Rule, so that the others may be warned.
• Moreover, a brother should not be in the company of 21
another at the wrong time.

Mar. 30
July 30
Nov. 29

• On Sunday all should give themselves to reading, 22
except those to whom other duties have been assigned.
• But if anyone is so careless and idle that he is either 23
unwilling or unable to study or read, he must be given
some other task so as not to be unemployed.
• To the brethren who are in poor health or not 24
strong, the work or craft that is allotted should be such
as to keep them occupied, but not such as by its weight to
break them down or drive them away. Their lack of 25
strength is a matter for the Abbot's consideration.

Chapter XLIX The Observance of Lent

1 • Although the monk's life ought at all seasons to bear a Mar. 31
2 Lenten character • such strength is found only in the few. July 31
Therefore we urge the brethren to keep the days of Lent Nov. 30
3 with a special purity of life • and also at this holy season
4 to make reparation for the failings of other times. • This
reparation will be worthily performed if we guard
ourselves from all our faults and apply ourselves to
prayer with tears, to reading, to compunction of heart
5 and to abstinence. • Therefore at this season let us
increase in some way the normal standard of our
service, as for example, by special prayers, or by a
6 diminution in food and drink; • and so let each one
spontaneously in the joy of the Holy Spirit[1] make some
offering to God concerning the allowance granted him.
7 • Thus he may reduce food and drink for his body, or his
sleep, or his talkativeness or his looseness in speech, and
so with the joy of spiritual desire, look forward to holy Easter.

8 • But every brother should propose to the Abbot
whatever he intends to offer, and it should be performed
9 with his blessing and approval. • For anything done
without the permission of the spiritual father will be put
down to presumption and vainglory, and deserving no
10 reward. • Everything, therefore, must be carried out with
the approval of the Abbot.

---

[1] cf. Rm 14:17

Chapter L Brethren who work far from the Oratory, or who are on a Journey

Apr. 1 Aug. 1 Dec. 1
• Brethren whose work is at a considerable distance, and 1
who cannot reach the oratory at the right time— • and 2
the Abbot recognises this to be the case— • should 3
perform the Work of God in the place where they are
working, kneeling down in deep respect to God. • And 4
likewise those who are travelling should not allow the
hours prescribed for prayer to go unobserved, but they
should do their best to carry out their duties in God's
service and not neglect them.

Chapter LI Brethren who go out on short Errands

1 • If a brother is sent out on some errand, and expects to Apr. 2
return to the monastery the same day, he must not Aug. 2
presume permission to eat outside the monastery, even if Dec. 2
2 the invitation is a very pressing one, • unless he has been
3 so instructed by the Abbot. • Anyone who does otherwise
is to be excommunicated.

Chapter LII The Oratory of the Monastery

Apr. 3 Aug. 3 Dec. 3 • The oratory should correspond to its name, and not be 1
used for any other purpose, nor to store things. • When 2
the Work of God has been completed all are to go out
noiselessly, and let reverence for God reign there. • So 3
that if a brother should have a mind to pray by himself,
he will not be disturbed by the ill-conduct of anyone else.
• Moreover, also on other occasions, if someone wishes to 4
make a private prayer, let him go in without hesitation
and pray, not, however, aloud, but with tears, and the
attention of his heart. • Anyone therefore, who is not 5
engaged on such a task, is not allowed to remain in the
oratory after the Work of God, as we said above, lest
someone else be disturbed.

Chapter LIII The Reception of Guests

1 • All who arrive as guests are to be welcomed like Christ, Apr. 4
for he is going to say, 'I was a stranger and you Aug. 4 Dec. 4
2 welcomed me.'[1] • The respect due to their station is to be
shown to all, particularly to those of one family with us in
3 the faith[2] and to pilgrims. • As soon as a guest is
announced he should be met by the superior or by
4 brethren with every expression of charity, • and first of
all they should pray together, and then greet one another
5 with the kiss of peace. • This kiss of peace should not be
offered until after prayer has been said, since the devil
6 sometimes plays tricks. • When guests arrive or depart
the greatest humility should be shown in addressing
7 them: • so, let Christ who is received in them be adored
with bowed head or prostrate body.

8 • So when the guests have been welcomed they
should be led to prayer, and then either the superior or
9 someone delegated by him should sit with them. • The
Divine Law should be read to them for their edification,
and after this every kindness should be shown to them.
10 • The superior may break the fast for the sake of a guest
unless it happens to be an important fast day which
11 cannot be waived; • the brethren, however, should keep
their accustomed fasts.

12 • The Abbot should give all the guests water to wash
13 their hands, • and with the whole community he should
14 wash their feet. • When they have done so, they should
recite the verse, *We have received your mercy, O God, in the
midst of your temple.*[3]

15 • Special care is to be shown in the reception of the

---

[1] Mt 25:35 [2] cf. Ga 6:10 [3] Ps 47:10

poor and of pilgrims, for in them especially is Christ
received; for the awe felt for the wealthy imposes respect
enough of itself.

Apr. 5 • The kitchen for the Abbot and guests should be 16
Aug. 5 separate, so that when guests arrive at unforeseeable
Dec. 5 times (and they are always coming to a monastery) they
may not disturb the brethren. • Two brethren capable of 17
performing this duty should take over this kitchen for a
year. • Help should be given them as they need it, so that 18
they may serve without complaining, and also, when
they have less work to do, they should leave their kitchen
to work wherever they are bidden. • And this principle 19
applies not only to them but to all departments of the
monastery: • help is to be provided for those in need, and 20
when they have spare time, they must obey their orders.

• Also, with regard to the guests' quarters, a brother 21
should be put in charge, whose soul is filled with the fear
of God. • A sufficient number of beds should be kept 22
ready there. And let God's house be wisely cared for by
wise men.

• No one without specific instructions is to associate or 23
converse with the guests. • If a brother should meet or 24
see one, he should, as we have said, give him a humble
greeting, and then ask a blessing and go on his way,
explaining that he is not allowed to converse with a
guest.

Chapter LIV Whether a Monk should receive Letters or other Gifts

1 • On no account may a monk, without the Abbot's Apr. 6 Aug. 6 Dec. 6
permission, either accept (or give) letters or offerings of
blessed bread or small gifts of any kind whether from his
2 parents or other people or his brethren. • And if
something is sent to him, even from his parents, he must
not take upon himself to accept it before it has been
3 shown to the Abbot. • If the Abbot allows it to be
accepted, it rests with him to decide to whom it shall be
4 given, • and the brother to whom it was sent must not be
5 upset, so that no opportunity is given the evil one. • If
anyone should be headstrong enough to act otherwise he
must submit to the discipline of the Rule.

Chapter LV The Clothing and Footwear of the Brethren

Apr. 7 • Clothing should be given to the brethren according to 1
Aug. 7 the nature of the district where they live and the climate,
Dec. 7 • because in cold places more is needed and in warm 2
ones less. • This is for the Abbot to consider. • It is our 3,4
view that in temperate localities, it will be sufficient for
monks if each has a cowl and a tunic— • the cowl should 5
be woolly in winter, but thin or worn in summer— • and 6
a scapular for work. For footwear he should have
stockings and shoes. • The monks should not argue 7
about the colour or coarseness of all these things, but
accept what is available in the region where they live or
can be bought cheaply.

• But the Abbot should take care about the size of 8
these clothes, that they are not too short for those who
use them, but of the right size. • Those who receive new 9
clothes should always give the old ones back at once;
they can be stored in the wardrobe for the benefit of the
poor. • For it is sufficient for a monk to have two tunics 10
and two cowls, to allow for wear at night and for
washing: • more than that is superfluous, and should be 11
taken away. • Their stockings also and anything that is 12
old should be returned by them when they get new ones.

• Those who are sent on a journey should get drawers 13
from the wardrobe, which they should wash and give
back on their return. • And their cowls and tunics 14
should be in rather better condition than those they
usually have; they should get them from the wardrobe
when they set out on this journey, and give them back on
their return.

15 • For bedding, a mattress, a blanket, a coverlet and a Apr. 8
16 pillow are enough. • The beds should be frequently Aug. 8 Dec. 8
inspected by the Abbot as a precaution against private
17 possessions. • If anyone is found to have anything which
was not given him by the Abbot, he is to undergo the
18 severest punishment; • and that this vice of personal
ownership may be totally eliminated, everything necessary
19 should be given by the Abbot; • namely, a cowl, a tunic,
stockings, shoes, a belt, a knife, a pen, a needle, a
handkerchief and writing tablets, so that all excuses
20 about necessity are removed. • But the Abbot must
always bear in mind the statement in the Acts of the
Apostles that 'distribution was made to each according
to his need.'[1]

21 • And so he must bear in mind the weakness of those
22 in need, but not the ill-will of the envious. • Indeed in all
his decisions he must consider that God will repay.

---

[1] Ac 4:35

Chapter LVI The Abbot's Table

Apr. 9 • The Abbot should always take his meals with the 1
Aug. 9
Dec. 9 guests and pilgrims. • Whenever there are no guests he 2
may at his own discretion invite to his table from among
the brethren those whom he wishes, • but one or two 3
seniors should always be left with the brethren for the
sake of discipline.

Chapter LVII The Craftsmen of the Monastery

1 • If there are craftsmen in the monastery let them carry Apr. 10
on their crafts in all humility, subject to the approval of Aug. 10 Dec. 10
2 the Abbot. • But if any one of them becomes conceited
because of his knowledge of his craft, which is
3 apparently bringing profit to the monastery, • he is to be
taken away from his craft; nor is he to come back to it,
unless, after he has shown humility, the Abbot gives him
4 a new permission. • If anything produced by the
craftsmen is to be sold, those responsible for the
transaction must take care not to venture to do anything
5 fraudulent. • They should always keep in mind the fate
of Ananias and Sapphira, lest the death which those
6 persons incurred in the body, • they (and any who
practise fraud in the affairs of the monastery) should
themselves undergo in their souls.

7 • With regard to the prices charged, the sin of avarice
8 must not creep in; • but whatever is sold should be a
9 little cheaper than is possible for lay-persons, • 'so that
God may be glorified in all things.'[1]

---

[1] I P 4:11

3
The Renovation of the Monastery

Chapter LVIII The Rules for receiving Brethren

1 • Easy admission is not to be granted to anyone as soon Apr. 11
2 as he applies to enter the monastic state, • but as the Aug. 11
Apostle says, 'Test the spirits to see whether they are of Dec. 11
3 God.'[1] • But if the newcomer continues to knock on the
door, and it is seen that he puts up patiently with the
unkind replies and the difficulty of getting in, and that
after four or five days he is still persisting in his request,
4 • then let him be allowed to come in, and remain in the
5 guest quarters for a few days. • After that he should be in
the quarters of the novices, where they work and eat and
6 sleep. • And to them should be assigned a senior monk
who has the gift of winning souls, and he should pay
7 them the closest attention. • His care must be to find out
whether the newcomer sincerely seeks God, whether he is
earnest at the Work of God, in obedience and under
8 severe words. • All the things that are hard and
repugnant to nature in the way to God are to be
expounded to him.

9 • If he promises to persevere in his intention to
remain, after two months have passed, this Rule is to be
10 read to him from beginning to end, • and he is to be told,
'This is the law under which you are asking to live. If you
can keep it, come in; if, however, you cannot, freely
11 depart.' • If he still stands his ground, then he is to be led
to the above-mentioned novices' quarter, and once again
his patience under all kinds of trials is to be put to the
12 test. • After the passing of another six months, the Rule
is to be read to him so that he may know what he is
13 entering on. • If he still remains, after four months the

[1] I Jn 4:1

same Rule is to be read to him again. • Then, if, having 14
thought the matter over carefully, he promises to keep all
the rules, and to obey all the orders given him, he should
be admitted into the community. • He must, however, 15
realise that it is set down in the law of the Rule that from
that day onward he may not leave the monastery, • nor 16
cast off from his neck the yoke of the Rule which it was
open to him during all this lengthy deliberation to
decline or to undertake.

Apr. 12 • The one who is to be accepted into the community 17
Aug. 12
Dec. 12 must promise in the oratory, in the presence of all,
stability, conversion of life and obedience. • He is to do 18
this before God and all his saints, so that if he
subsequently behaves otherwise, he will know that he merits
condemnation by him the one whom he mocks. • With 19
regard to this promise he must write a petition, calling
on the names of the saints whose relics are there, and in
the name of the Abbot who is present. • This petition he 20
should write with his own hand or, if he is illiterate, it
must be written by another whom he has asked, and the
novice must make his sign on it. And he should place it
with his own hand on the altar. • When he has done so, 21
the novice himself straight away intones this verse, *Accept
me, Lord, according to your word, and I shall live, and you will
not disappoint me in my hope.*[2] • The whole community 22
repeats this verse three times, adding *Glory be to the Father*
at the end. • Then the brother novice prostrates himself 23
at the feet of each of the brethren, asking their prayers.
Then from that day onwards he is to be reckoned among
the community. • If he has any possessions, he must 24
either previously give them to the poor, or by means of a
formal donation give them to the monastery, keeping for

[2] Ps 118:116

25 himself nothing at all, • since he realises that from that
26 day he will have no power even over his own body. • At
once then in the oratory, let him be stripped of his own
clothes which he is wearing, and reclothed in those of the
27 monastery. • The clothes, however, which have been
taken from him must be placed in the wardrobe, and kept
28 there, • so that if at some later time he should agree to
the suggestion of the devil that he should leave the
monastery (which God forbid), he can be stripped of the
29 clothing of the monastery, before being sent away. • He
does not, however, get back the petition which the Abbot
took off the altar, but it is kept in the monastery.

Chapter LIX The Sons of the Rich or the Poor who are offered

Apr. 13 Aug. 13 Dec. 13

• If it happens that a nobleman offers his son to God as a 1
monk, and the child is still of tender age, the parents
should make out the petition of which we have spoken.
• They should wrap this petition and the boy's hand 2
together with the Mass offering in the altar cloth and
offer him in that way. • As for their property, they must 3
in the same petition promise under oath that on no
occasion will they ever give him anything either
themselves or through an agent or by any other means,
nor will they afford him any opportunity for possessing
anything. • However, if they are unwilling to do this, and 4
want to have the merit of giving something as an alms to
the monastery, • they should make a donation to the 5
monastery of whatever they want to give; they may
reserve the income of it to themselves if they wish. • Thus 6
will be blocked every way by which expectation might
remain to deceive the child and (God forbid), lead him to
destruction, as we have learnt by experience.

• And poorer people may follow the same procedure. 7
• As for those who possess nothing at all, they may 8
simply make the petition and offer their son with the
Mass offering in the presence of witnesses.

Chapter LX Priests who may want to live in the Monastery

1 • If anyone of the rank of priest asks to be taken into the Apr. 14
monastery, this should not be granted him too quickly. Aug. 14 Dec. 14
2 • If, however, he is very persistent in his request, he must
understand that he will have to observe the full discipline
3 of the Rule • and that no relaxation will be made for him,
as the Scripture says, 'Friend, for what purpose have you
4 come?'[1] • Nevertheless it may be granted him to stand
next to the Abbot, to pronounce blessings, and to
celebrate Mass, provided the Abbot gives permission.
5 • Otherwise he must not take any privilege for granted,
knowing that he is subject to the discipline of the Rule,
and should give greater proofs of humility to all.
6 • Moreover, in the event of some appointment or other
7 monastic business coming up for consideration, • he
must keep the position in the community which goes
with the date of his entry into the monastery, and not the
one granted him out of reverence for the priesthood.

8 • If any clerics should show the same desire to join the monastery, they should be placed in a slightly advanced position in the community, and they, too, must promise observance of the Rule and stability.

[1] Mt 26:50

Chapter LXI How Travelling Monks are to be received

Apr. 15 • If a travelling monk should arrive from some far-off 1
Aug. 15
Dec. 15 locality, and want to live as a guest in the monastery,
• and be content with the customs that he finds there, 2
and not disturb the community by making special
demands, • but be quite content with what he finds, then 3
let him be accepted for as long as he desires. • And if 4
indeed with humble charity he reasonably criticises or
points some things out, the Abbot should consider the
matter carefully. For it may be that the Lord has sent
him for this very purpose. • And if later on he wants to 5
settle down permanently, this desire is not to be refused,
especially as his way of life could be well known during
his time as a guest.

Apr. 16 • If on the other hand during that time, he should be 6
Aug. 16
Dec. 16 found demanding or a man of bad habits, not only
should he not be allowed to join the community, • but he 7
should be frankly told to go away, for fear that others
should be corrupted by his unhappy condition.

• If, however, he is not the kind which deserves 8
dismissal, not only should he be admitted to the
community if he so petitions, • but he should be 9
persuaded to stay so that others may be instructed by his
example, • and because it is the one Lord we serve in 10
every place, and the one King for whom the battle is
fought. • Indeed if the Abbot sees him to be of sufficeint 11
virtue, he may place him in a somewhat higher position.
• In fact the Abbot may assign a more honourable 12
position than that due to the day of entry not only to a
monk, but to one coming from the above-mentioned

ranks of priests or clerics, if he recognises that their way
13 of life is worthy of such treatment. • The Abbot, however, must take care never to accept permanently a monk from another known monastery without either the agreement of his Abbot or a letter of recommendation,
14 • since it is written, 'Do not to another what you would not want done to yourself.'[1]

[1] Tb 4:16

Chapter LXII The Priests of the Monastery

Apr. 17 • If an Abbot wishes to have a priest or deacon ordained 1
Aug. 17
Dec. 17 for his service, he should choose from his monks one who
is fit to exercise the priesthood. • He who is ordained, 2
however, must beware of elation or pride • and he should 3
not take upon himself any work that has not been
committed to him by the Abbot.

He should realise that he is all the more bound to
submit to monastic discipline. • Nor on account of his 4
priesthood should he forget the obedience and the
discipline of the Rule, but he should go forward more
and more towards God.

• Let him always keep the position corresponding to 5
his entry into the monastery, • except when officiating at 6
the altar, unless the choice of the community and the will
of the Abbot promote him to a higher station on account
of the merit of his life. • He should realise that he is 7
bound by the rule laid down for deans and priors; • if he 8
presumes to behave otherwise, the judgement will be
passed not *on the priest but on the rebellion.* • If after 9
frequent warnings he does not mend his ways, the Bishop
also should be called in as a witness against him. • If, 10
even so, he does not amend and his faults are manifest,
he must be expelled from the monastery—• that is if his 11
stubbornness is such that he will neither submit nor obey
the Rule.

Chapter LXIII The Order of the Community

1 • The time of their entering monastic life, their personal Apr. 18 Aug. 18
merits, and the decision of the Abbot, shall decide the Dec. 18
2 order which they keep in the monastery. • Yet the Abbot
must not upset the flock entrusted to him, nor should he
make any unjust arrangement as though he were free to
3 give orders as he pleases, • for he must always bear in
mind that he is going to have to render an account of all
4 his decisions and actions. • In the order, then, which he
has laid down, or which they otherwise have among
themselves, shall the brethren come to the kiss of peace,
or to Communion, or intone a Psalm or occupy their
5 place in choir. • In no circumstances or places is age to
6 decide order or have any bearing upon it, • for the
youthful Samuel and Daniel acted as judges over their
7 elders. • Therefore, with the exception of those whom, as
we have said, the Abbot has promoted or degraded for
definite reasons, the rest are to take their places
according to the time of their coming to the monastery;
8 • for example, one who has entered the monastery at the
second hour is to know that he is junior to him who
9 entered at the first, whatever his age or dignity. • For the
boys, however, all have the task of keeping order
wherever they are.

10 • Juniors, therefore, must show respect for their Apr. 19 Aug. 19
11 seniors, and seniors must love their juniors. • In calling Dec. 19
one another by name it is not allowed to anyone to use
12 the name alone • seniors should address their juniors by
the name of brother; juniors should address their seniors
as *Nonnus*, by which is signified the reverence due to a
13 father. • The Abbot, however, as he is believed to act in

the place of Christ, should be called Lord and Abbot, not because he demands these titles, but for the honour and love of Christ. • He himself must bear this in mind, 14
and show himself worthy of such honour.

• Whenever the brethren meet one another, the junior 15
should seek a blessing of the elder. • A younger monk 16
should rise and offer the seat to an older one if he passes by, nor should he venture to sit down again, unless the older one tells him to, • so that it may be as it is written, 17
'Forestall one another in paying honour.'[1]

• Children and youths are to keep their places, in good 18
order, in the oratory and at table. • Out of doors also and 19
anywhere at all they should be under supervision and discipline, until they reach an age that can understand.

[1] Rm 12:10

Chapter LXIV The Institution of the Abbot

1 • This principle must always be kept in mind in the Apr. 20
institution of the Abbot: he should be appointed whom Aug. 20
the united community chooses in the fear of God, or Dec. 20
whom a smaller part of the community chooses with the
2 sounder judgement. • He who is to be appointed must be
chosen on account of his virtuous life and wise teaching,
3 even if he is the last in order in the community. • So that
even if (may it not happen!) the whole community
should with one accord elect a person who will connive at
4 their defects, • and if these defects somehow become
known to the Bishop to whose diocese the place belongs,
5 and to the local abbots or christians, • they should put a
stop to this plot of wicked men, and set a worthy steward
6 over the household of God. • And they should know that
they will receive a good reward if they act with a pure
intention and zeal for God, and that on the other hand it
would be sinful to neglect their duty.

7 • When he has been instituted, the Abbot should Apr. 21
always bear in mind what a burden he has undertaken, Aug. 21
and to whom he will have to render an account of his Dec. 21
8 stewardship. • He should know, too, that he ought to be
of profit to his brethren rather than just preside over
9 them. • He ought, therefore, to be learned in the divine
law, so that he may know it well, and that it may be for
him a store whence he draws forth new things and old.
He should be a chaste man, temperate and merciful.
10 • He should always prefer mercy to judgement,[1] that he
11 may also obtain mercy. • Let him hate sin, let him love
the brethren.

[1] Jm 2:13

• In correcting he should act prudently, and not 12
overdo it; for fear that as he tries too hard to get rid of the
rust, the pot gets broken. • Also he should always 13
mistrust his own frailty, and remember that the bruised
reed is not to be broken. • In saying these things, we do 14
not imply that he should allow vices to flourish, but that
he should eliminate them prudently and with charity, as
seems best in each case, as we have already said. • And it 15
should be his aim to be loved rather than feared. • Let 16
him not be restless or anxious, not over-demanding and
obstinate, not a perfectionist or full of suspicion, or he
will never have any peace. • In giving his instructions he 17
should have forethought and consideration; and whether
the instructions which he gives concern God's affairs or
temporal ones, let him be discerning and moderate,
• bearing in mind the discretion of holy Jacob who said, 18
'If I cause my flocks to be overdriven, they will all die in
one day.'[2]

• Taking to heart therefore these and other examples 19
of discretion, the mother of virtues, he should so regulate
everything that the strong may desire to carry more, and
the weak are not afraid.

• And, especially, he must in every respect keep this 20
present Rule • so that having fulfilled his ministry well, 21
he may hear from the Lord the same words as that good
servant who gave his fellow servants wheat in due
season, • 'Truly I say to you, he will place him over 22
everything he owns.'[3]

---

[2] Gn 33:13 [3] Mt 24:47

Chapter LXV The Prior of the Monastery

1 • It happens fairly often that serious scandals occur in Apr. 22
2 monasteries because of the appointment of a Prior; • for Aug. 22 Sept. 22
there are those who, swelling up with an evil spirit of
pride, consider themselves second abbots, act like tyrants
and nourish scandals and quarrels in the community.
3 • This happens especially in places where the Prior is
appointed by the same Bishop or by the same abbots as
4 appoint the Abbot of the monastery. • It is easy to see
how unwise this is: for from the very beginning of his
appointment the Prior is given grounds for waxing
5 proud, • since his thoughts suggest to him that he is
6 exempt from the Abbot's authority, because, • 'You have
been appointed by the same persons as the Abbot.'
7 • Hence arise envy, quarrels, detraction, rivalries, dis-
8 sensions and disorders; • for while the Abbot and Prior
are in opposition to each other, of necessity their own
9 souls are endangered by this quarrelling, • and also those
under their authority, seeking favour from one side or the
10 other, head for perdition. • The evils arising from such a
dangerous state of affairs are due primarily to those who
have been the originators of such a disorder.

11 • For this reason we think it expedient for the Apr. 23
preservation of peace and charity that the making of Aug. 23 Dec. 23
appointments in the monastery should depend on the
12 Abbot's judgement • and, if it is possible, that all the
business of the monastery should be carried on through
deans, under the control of the Abbot, as we have
13 already laid down. • Thus no one may wax proud over
what is committed to many.

14 • If, however, local conditions require it, or the

community makes a reasonable and humble request, and
the Abbot judges it to be expedient, • then the Abbot 15
himself should appoint as his Prior whomsoever he
chooses after taking the advice of God-fearing brethren.
• For his part the Prior is to perform respectfully 16
whatever functions the Abbot lays upon him, and do
nothing contrary to his will or arrangements. • For 17
inasmuch as he has been placed over others, he should
the more carefully keep the precepts of the Rule. • If it 18
should turn out that the Prior has serious faults or,
deceived by vanity, acts arrogantly, or it turns out that
he is a belittler of the Holy Rule, he should be verbally
rebuked up to four times; • if he does not then change his 19
ways, he should be punished according to the disciplinary code. • If, however, he does not amend even so, 20
then he must be deposed from his office as Prior, and
another who is suitable for it be put in his place. • And if 21
afterwards he does not live quietly and obediently among
the community, he should even be expelled from the
monastery.

• The Abbot should, however, bear in mind the 22
account he must render to God for all his decisions, for
fear that the flame of jealousy or evil zeal burn in his
soul.

Chapter LXVI The Doorkeepers of the Monastery

1 • At the gate of the monastery, a wise old man is to be Apr. 24
posted, one capable of receiving a message and giving a Aug. 24 Dec. 24
reply, and whose maturity guarantees that he will not
2 wander round. • This doorkeeper should have a cell near
the gate, so that persons who arrive may always find
3 someone at hand to give them a reply. • As soon as
anyone knocks, or a poor man calls out, he should
4 answer 'Thanks be to God' or 'God bless you'. • Then
with all the gentleness that comes from the fear of God,
he should speedily and with the warmth of charity attend
to the enquirer.

5 • If the doorkeeper needs it, he should have a younger
brother to help him.

6 • If it is possible, the monastery should be organised so
that all its needs, that is to say things such as water, a
mill, a garden, and various crafts, may be met within its
7 premises, • so that the monks have no need to wander
round outside it, for that does not profit their souls at all.
8 • This Rule we wish to be read frequently in the
community, so that none of the brethren may plead
ignorance of it.

Appendix

Chapter LXVII Brethren sent on a Journey

1 • Brethren who are being sent on a journey are to commend themselves to the prayers of all the brethren Apr. 25 Aug. 25 Dec. 25
2 and of the Abbot; • and in the final prayer of the Work of God there should be a commemoration of all who are
3 absent. • When brethren return from a journey, at all the canonical hours of the day on which they return, they should lie prostrate on the floor of the oratory, as the
4 Work of God comes to an end, • and ask for the prayers of all,[1] for any faults that may have overtaken them on their journey, such as the sight or hearing of an evil thing
5 or idle chatter. • No one should venture to tell another anything he may have seen or heard while outside the
6 monastery, for that does much harm. • But if anyone does this he must undergo punishment according to the
7 Rule. • The same thing applies to anyone who dares to go out of the enclosure of the monastery, or to go anywhere, or do anything, although of small importance, without the approval of the Abbot.

---

[1] cf Tb 11:7 (Vulg.)

Chapter LXVIII If a Brother is set impossible Tasks

Apr. 26 • If it should happen that burdensome or impossible 1
Aug. 26
Dec. 26 tasks are imposed on one of the brethren he should
indeed accept with complete calm and obedience the
command of the one who so orders, • but if he sees that 2
the weight of the burden quite exceeds the limits of his
strength, he should quietly and at a suitable moment
explain to his superior the reasons why he cannot do it,
• not in a proud way nor with the spirit of resistance, or 3
contradiction. • But if after his explanations the one in 4
authority remains firm in requiring what he has ordered,
the junior must understand that this is what is best for
him, • and let him lovingly trust in God's aid, and so 5
obey.

Chapter LXIX That in the Monastery one must not defend another

1 • Let it be noted that in the monastery no monk may assume the right to defend or act as a kind of protector to Apr. 27 Aug. 27 Dec. 27
2 another for any reason whatever, • even if they are
3 connected by a bond blood-relationship. • Monks must not presume to do this in any way, for from it may arise the
4 possibility of very grave scandals. • If anyone offends in this respect he must be sharply dealt with.

Chapter LXX That no one may hit another

Apr. 28 • All outbreaks of self-assertiveness are to be avoided in 1
Aug. 28
Dec. 28 the monastery. • We therefore lay down that no one is 2
allowed to excommunicate or strike any of his brethren,
unless the Abbot has given him authority to do so.
• 'Those who offend must be rebuked in the presence of 3
all, so that the rest may be warned.'[1] • Care, however, 4
and supervision are to be shown by everyone with regard
to the discipline of children up to fifteen years of age,
• yet with all moderation and good sense. • With regard 5 6
to those who are older than that, if anyone presumes to
take action without the Abbot's instruction, or gets angry
and behaves without discretion to the children also, he
must submit to the discipline of the Rule, • for it is 7
written, 'Do not to another what you would not have
done to yourself.'[2]

[1]Tm 5:20 [2]Tb 4:16

Chapter LXXI That the Brethren obey one another

1 • The goodness of obedience is not to be shown only Apr. 29
through obedience to the Abbot, but the brethren should Aug. 29 Dec. 29
2 also obey each other, • in the knowledge that by this path
3 of obedience they will draw nearer God. • The commands
of the Abbot or of the superiors appointed by him must
come first and we do not allow personal demands to be
4 attended to before them, • but otherwise all the younger
monks should obey the older ones with all love and care.
5 • And if anyone is found to be contentious, he should be
6 corrected. • And if, for any reason at all, a brother is
7 corrected in any way by the Abbot or by an elder, • or if
he perceives that the feelings of any elder have been
8 roused to anger against him, even slightly, • he should at
once and without delay prostrate himself at his feet and
lie there in sign of reparation until the rift is healed by a
9 blessing. • If anyone is too proud to do this, he must
either undergo corporal punishment or, if he is contumacious, he must be put out of the monastery.

Chapter LXXII On the good Zeal which Monks ought to have

Apr. 30 Aug. 30 Dec. 30 • As there is an evil zeal rooted in bitterness which 1
separates from God and leads to hell, • so there is a good 2
zeal which separates from vice and leads to God and to
eternal life. • This, therefore, is the zeal which monks 3
should practise with the most ardent love, • in other 4
words, they should forestall one another in paying
honour.[1] • They should with the greatest patience make 5
allowance for one another's weaknesses, whether physical
or moral. • They should rival one another in practising 6
obedience. • No one should pursue what he thinks 7
advantageous for himself, but rather what seems best for
another. • They should labour with chaste love at the 8
charity of the brotherhood. • They should fear God. 9
• They should love their Abbot with sincere and humble 10
charity. • They should prefer nothing whatever to 11
Christ.

• May he bring us all alike to life everlasting. 12

---

[1] Rm 12:10

Epilogue

Chapter LXXIII That the whole Keeping of Justice[1] is not covered by this Rule

May 1 • We have written this Rule so that by following it in 1
Aug. 31 Dec. 31 monasteries, we may to some extent show that we lead
blameless lives and possess a beginning of the monastic
way of life. • In addition there are for him who would 2
hasten to the perfection of the monastic ways the
doctrines of the holy Fathers, which, if a man keeps
them, will lead to the height of perfection. • For is not 3
every page of the Old or New Testament, every word of
the Divine Author, a most direct rule for our human life?
• Does not every book of the Catholic Fathers proclaim 4
that we should make our way by the most direct path to
our Creator? • There are also the *Conferences*, and 5
Institutes, and the *Lives of the Fathers*, and the *Rule* of the
holy Father Basil. • What are these works but aids to the 6
attainment of virtue for good-living and obedient monks?
• But to us who are slothful, who live badly and who are 7
negligent, they bring a blush of shame. • Whoever you 8
are, then, who are hurrying forward to your heavenly
fatherland, do you with Christ's help fulfil this little Rule
written for beginners; • and then you will come at the 9
end, under God's protection, to those heights of learning
and virtue which we have mentioned above. Amen.

[1] Cf. Mt 3:15

Milton Keynes UK
Ingram Content Group UK Ltd.
UKHW041910040924
447908UK00004B/9

9 781781 820186